ON THE COUCH

ON THE COUCH

A Repressed History of
the Analytic Couch
from Plato to Freud

Nathan Kravis

The MIT Press
Cambridge, Massachusetts
London, England

This book was set in PF Din Pro by the MIT Press. Printed and bound in Spain.

Library of Congress Cataloging-in-Publication Data

Names: Kravis, Nathan, author.
Title: On the couch : a repressed history of the analytic couch from Plato to Freud / Nathan Kravis.
Description: Cambridge, MA : The MIT Press, [2017] | Includes bibliographical references and index.
Identifiers: LCCN 2016052900 | ISBN 9780262036610 (hardcover : alk. paper)
Subjects: | MESH: Psychoanalysis--history | Psychotherapeutic Processes | Interior Design and Furnishings--history | Patient Positioning | Professional-Patient Relations
Classification: LCC RC506 | NLM WM 11.1 | DDC 616.89/17--dc23 LC record available at
    https://lccn.loc.gov/2016052900

10 9 8 7 6 5 4 3 2 1

for Leora

Socrates to Strepsiades:
Just lie down there ...
And try and think out one of your
own problems.

**Aristophanes, *The Clouds* (423 BCE),
trans. A. H. Sommerstein**

Contents

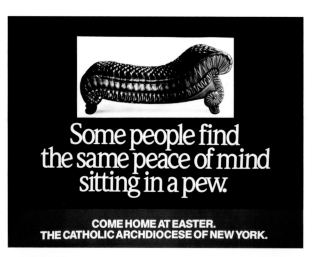

0.1 and 0.2
New York City subway posters, 1991.

Preface

I began dreaming of writing *On the Couch* twenty-five years ago when, as a candidate in psychoanalytic training, I journeyed by subway four times a week to my analyst's office to lie on his couch. It's hard to say how many times I stood on the subway platform staring at one of those huge, glossy posters with the image of an analytic couch before I could finally begin to formulate my thoughts about what it was doing there. These enormous couch posters in the New York City subway system were part of an advertising campaign by the Archdiocese of New York. They bore the caption (some in English, others in Spanish), "Some people find the same peace of mind sitting in a pew. Come home at Easter. The Catholic Archdiocese of New York" (see figures 0.1 and 0.2).

These advertisements were obviously not aimed at psychoanalytic trainees like me. Who, I wondered, comprised the target audience? And why was the Church so confident that subway riders would easily decode the image in front of them, and immediately understand the implied choice between couch and pew?

As I mulled these questions over, I contacted the Archdiocese to say I was interested in writing about the couch, and would they be so kind as to send me copies of these subway images? I was referred to the advertising agency retained by the Church, and soon I was the gleeful recipient of a long, narrow cardboard box containing two posters, each six feet wide by four feet high, one in English, the other in Spanish. So began the long gestation of *On the Couch.*

Over the years, as I clipped one *New Yorker* cartoon after another and read everything I could find in the psychoanalytic literature about the couch, I slowly began to realize that the disjuncture between the couch's impressive iconic significance and the dearth of analytic writing about its role in clinical analysis should be the starting point of my inquiry. I wanted to write not about analytic technique but about the origins of its very odd choreography—a supine person speaking to an unseen seated one. Here the psychoanalytic literature falls almost completely silent.

So I looked elsewhere. In researching what I came to think of as the "repressed" history of the analytic couch, I was drawn into art history, furniture history, fashion and clothing history, as well as works on classical antiquity and modern art.

Meanwhile, my already-bulging folder of favorite couch cartoons from the *New Yorker* was further stretched with the addition of images from magazine covers, newspaper stories, catalogs, and advertisements. The result is a multidisciplinary effort that I hope engages readers with a wide range of interests. *On the Couch* is a book that has a natural audience among devotees of the so-called *psy* disciplines[1] (psychiatry, psychology, and psychoanalysis) and, more broadly, anyone intrigued by the setting and procedure of "talk therapy." But it also speaks to students and practitioners of furniture history and design, interior decoration, art, and cultural studies.

Whereas previous examinations of the origins of the use of the couch have not looked past Freud, *On the Couch* shows how Freud's analytic setup cannot be adequately understood without situating it in its complex cultural context. Convergences of social mores with respect to manners, clothing, and deportment, as well as furniture innovation and evolving medical treatment ideals and exigencies, are illustrated and newly probed. Freud's determination that psychoanalysis is best conducted with the analyst seated out of sight behind the recumbent analysand is related to this nexus of cultural, aesthetic, and medical and psychiatric traditions. With a combination of sumptuous imagery and critical commentary, I have sought to bring forward a fuller appreciation of the ways Freud shaped and was shaped by these traditions in *On the Couch*.

Since office furnishings and décor inevitably reflect the analyst's participation in a timeless discourse about the meanings of appearance, the analytic community itself comes under scrutiny in *On the Couch*. However mightily today's analysts strive to distance themselves from Freud's archaeologically inflected and Romantic consultation-room motifs, they find themselves enacting one aspect or another of an endless debate about what furnishings and décor reveal about moral and social values. *On the Couch* shows how contemporary analysts are unconscious carriers of split representations of the couch, and of the psychoanalytic enterprise in general.

On the Couch describes not only the evolution of the couch from the bed, the bench, the settee, the *chaise-longue*, and the sofa, but also its embeddedness in our society's cultural imagination. The analytic couch has become an icon that transcends psychoanalysis itself insofar as it stands in the popular imagination as a symbol of interiority, self-knowledge, and mental healing even to those who have no particular interest in treatment. *On the Couch* explains how and why psycho-analysts themselves are ambivalent about the couch's protean symbolic stature.

As a practicing psychoanalyst, I find the dialogue between the rich iconography of the couch and its debated clinical utility endlessly captivating. I hope that *On the Couch* will invite readers with widely varied interests to share that fascination.

New York, 2016

Acknowledgments

I am fortunate to have found an intellectual home at the DeWitt Wallace Institute for the History of Psychiatry in the Department of Psychiatry at Weill Cornell Medical College. My colleagues there have immeasurably enriched my work, and have been a steady source of stimulation and encouragement over the past thirty years. I am especially indebted to George Makari and Leonard Groopman for their thoughtful comments on earlier drafts of this book. Thanks also to Lawrence Friedman, Robert Michels, Katherine Dalsimer, Daria Colombo, Nirav Soni, Hilary Beattie, Rosemary Stevens, Theodore Shapiro, Aaron Esman, Barbara Stimmel, Orna Ophir, Anne Hoffman, and Megan Wolff. I owe a special debt of gratitude to Marisa Shaari, the Special Collections Librarian of the Oskar Diethelm Library at the History of Psychiatry Institute, for her research assistance as well as for her unflaggingly good-natured general helpfulness. Other colleagues in the Cornell psychiatry department, especially my erstwhile co-teacher Elizabeth Auchincloss, have provided invaluable mentoring, friendship, and support over these many years.

The Columbia University Center for Psychoanalytic Training and Research has been a second home, and a place where deep and wide-ranging curiosity and passionate engagement with learning have always been highly valued. My thanks to my teachers and colleagues there, and to the many outstanding candidates in psychoanalytic training I have had the privilege to teach and supervise for the past twenty-five years.

A book like *On the Couch* cannot be realized without help from a wide variety of scholars, librarians, curators, artists, and the resources of many collections. An incomplete list of those who deserve mention follows: Eric Anderson and Mary Bergstein, Department of the History of Art and Visual Culture at the Rhode Island School of Design (RISD); Claudia Covert and Ariel Bordeaux, the Fleet Library of RISD; Phyllis Magidson, Museum of the City of New York; Patricia Kuharic, Medical Art and Photography, Weill Cornell Medical College; Arlene Shaner, New York Academy of Medicine; Rhoda Bawdekar of the International Psychoanalytic Association, London; Shellburne Thurber; Guy Billout; and Willhemina Wahlin of Charles Sturt University, Australia.

Anne Edelstein, my agent, went well above and beyond the call of duty in seeing this book through from start to finish. Roger Conover and his dream team at the MIT Press, including Margarita Encomienda, Matthew Abbate, Gillian Beaumont, Janet Rossi, David Ryman, and Victoria Hindley, managed to be both meticulous and creative in editing and designing this book. Their expertise and diligence have greatly enhanced the final product.

To thank Leora Kahn for her indefatigable efforts on my behalf in illustration research and image procurement would be to seriously understate my indebtedness to her. When this book was at a much earlier and uncertain stage of development, she pushed for its realization, and it never could have been completed without her. An author is lucky indeed when love so liberally encompasses visual imagination and promotes the fulfilment of literary desire.

Why Is the Couch Used in Psychoanalysis?

Most psychoanalysts today are ambivalent about the couch, ignorant of its provenance, and unable to state a compelling clinical rationale for its earliest use. Yet the analytic couch is universally understood to represent psychoanalysis, and is a widely recognized icon of self-knowledge. How can we understand the origins of its use?

Psychoanalysts can't be blamed for being in the dark about the origins of the use of the couch. Although the analytic couch is the principal and uncontested iconic fixture of their profession, the story of its provenance is a complicated one. It defies simply stated histories of analytic technique, and it plunges practitioners of an already embattled treatment modality into a murky narrative concerning something about which many of them feel defensive or skeptical. After all, the use of the couch in psychoanalysis is unstudied. There is no substantial body of empirical research on posture, frequency of sessions, or duration of psychoanalytic treatment.[1] For a variety of reasons—confidentiality, methodologic problems, lack of funding—clinical research in psychoanalysis is devilishly difficult to conduct. While many in the field are now working hard to correct this deficit, in general analysts have had to rely on clinical tradition and their own personal and clinical experiences to guide them when it comes to crucial questions of technique.

In the absence of empirical research findings, most analysts seek support for their techniques in clinical lore and theories of therapeutic action. But given the couch's iconic status, its use is strangely undertheorized. This is even more surprising when one considers the fact that analysts have often been chided for their readiness to construct theories about almost anything.

Freud famously said that he got patients to lie on a couch because he couldn't stand being stared at all day.[2] That's not much of a theory of technique. It is, one could argue, a *proto*-theory in the sense that it is perhaps the germ of a line of thinking about the advantages *for the analyst* of the patient's use of the couch—a line that led ultimately to Bion's work on the analyst's capacity for reverie and containment.[3] Still, it should be acknowledged that if the analyst's goal is not to be stared at, or to be freed from attending to visual social cues so as to be better able to access her own reverie, she could arrange the chairs so that she and her patient are not face to face. That, in fact, is exactly what was eventually done by the British object relations theorist W. R. D. Fairbairn, and other analysts who rose to prominence after Freud's death in 1939, including (in the U.S.) Harry Stack Sullivan,

1.1
Sigmund Freud (1856–1939), 1909.

Erich Fromm, Frieda Fromm-Reichmann, and Clara Thompson.[4] Clearly, Freud saw that the patient's recumbence was beneficial to him in his functioning as an analyst, but he didn't articulate this as a reason for all analysts to require the use of the couch, and, as noted, he didn't explain what would distinguish this practice from, for example, having the patient sit in a chair facing away from the analyst.

And if the idea is to enhance the patient's capacity for free association, why wouldn't the analyst try to analyze whatever inhibits free-associating rather than intervene with an action such as a directive about posture?

In short, the stated reasons for the use of the couch don't make sense. This doesn't mean that its use is a bad idea. It's unquestionably helpful to the *analyst*, it provides the analysand with a unique experience, and there may even be something about the psychophysiology of recumbence (as yet unknown to us) that makes it beneficial to them as well.[5] But it is odd that something as iconic as the couch should be so underrepresented in psychoanalytic theories of technique. Freud stipulated the use of the couch *before* anyone elaborated any real rationale.[6] Yet the couch quickly became an emblem of orthodoxy, initially in contradistinction to Jungian and Adlerian practitioners,[7] but then continuously for subsequent generations of analysts ever since, and a widely recognized icon of psychoanalysis (see figures 1.2 and 1.3).

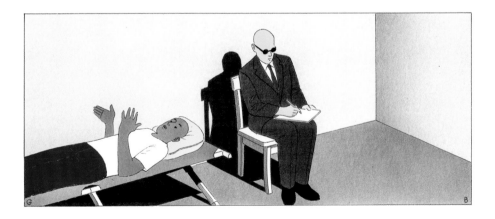

1.2
New Yorker illustration, 2006.

4

FEBRUARY 5, 2007

NEW YORK

CENTRAL PARK NORTH THE LAST MANHATTAN **REAL-ESTATE STEAL**

How Are You Feeling, Mr. President?

Probing the psyche
of the loneliest decider since
Richard Nixon.

By John
Heilemann
plus Robert Stone,
Deepak Chopra,
Christopher Buckley,
Peter Kramer,
Dahlia Lithwick,
Melvin Laird,
and other students
of narcissism,
delusion,
abandonment...

1.3
New York magazine cover, 2007.

Within the profession, the couch has been both fetishized as talismanic and disparaged as infantilizing.[8] Many analysts today regard it as nonessential; most (if not all) would agree that its use is no guarantor of an analytic process.[9] Some have even scoffed at the tradition of the patient's recumbence, seeing it as a relic of a more authoritarian era, a power play on the part of the analyst that unnecessarily regresses or infantilizes the analysand.[10] Nevertheless, the couch was precociously identified as a distinctive feature of psychoanalysis, and was thought to represent something essential about the analytic enterprise and process, whence its metonymic and synecdochic (i.e., "on the couch" became a way of saying "in analysis") status.[11] Examples of this synecdoche could be endlessly multiplied, but a few illustrations will suffice to make the point: the couch *signifies* analysis to analysts and nonanalysts alike—in this instance to mental health professionals (figure 1.4), to the *New York Times* readership (figure 1.5), and to the general public (figure 1.6).

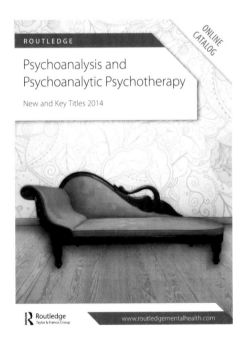

1.4
Routledge book catalog, 2014.

IDEAS & TRENDS

Freud Is Widely Taught at Universities, Except in the Psychology Department

By PATRICIA COHEN

PSYCHOANALYSIS and its ideas about the unconscious mind have spread to every nook and cranny of the culture from Salinger to "South Park," from Fellini to foreign policy. Yet if you want to learn about psychoanalysis at the nation's top universities, one of the last places to look may be the psychology department.

A new report by the American Psychoanalytic Association has found that while psychoanalysis — or what purports to be psychoanalysis — is alive and well in literature, film, history and just about every other subject in the humanities, psychology departments and textbooks treat it as "desiccated and dead," a historical artifact instead of "an ongoing movement and a living, evolving process."

The study, which is to appear in the June 2008 issue of psychiatry's flagship journal, The American Journal of Psychiatry, is the latest evidence of the field's existential crisis. For decades now, critics engaged in the Freud Wars have pummeled the good doctor's theories for being sexist, fraudulent, unscientific, or just plain wrong. In their eyes, psychoanalysis belongs with discarded practices like leeching.

But to beleaguered psychoanalysts who have lost ground to other forms of therapy that promise quicker results through cheaper and easier methods, the report underscores pressing questions about the relevance of their field and whether it will survive as a practice.

Given how psychoanalytic ideas have shaped the culture, the issue reverberates far beyond the tiny cluster of psychoanalysts. They worry that the gradual disappearance of psychoanalytic theory from psychology curriculums means that those ideas are bound to be applied incorrectly as new advances are neglected.

These worries led the psychoanalytic association to create a task force to increase undergraduates' exposure to psychoanalytic ideas as both a theory and therapy.

The effort includes this new study, a computer-based analysis of course descriptions at 150 public and private institu-

PAUL HOPPE

1.5
New York Times illustration, 2007.

Beyond its status as a synecdoche for all of psychoanalysis, the analytic couch has entered the public lexicon of cultural icons for self-awareness.

Obviously, recumbence is associated with a panoply of activities: sex, sleep, birth, death, sickness, healing, reading, and repose—some or all of which may be evoked by the use of the couch in psychoanalytic treatment. But what determined its selection as quintessential and paradigmatic in psychoanalysis *before* its use could even begin to be theorized?

To begin to frame a response to this question, let's look at what Freud actually said about requiring the use of the couch:

> I must say a word about a certain *ceremonial* which concerns the position in which the treatment is carried out. I hold to the plan of getting the patient to lie on a sofa [*Ruhebett*] while I sit behind him out of his sight. This arrangement has a historical basis; it is the *remnant* of the hypnotic method out of which psycho-analysis was evolved. But it deserves to be maintained for many reasons. The first is a personal motive, but one which others may share with me. I cannot put up with being stared at by other people for eight hours a day (or more). ... I insist on this procedure ... to isolate the transference and to allow it to come forward in due course sharply defined as a resistance.[12]

1.6
De Beers diamond advertisement, 1996.

Leaving aside, for the moment, this questionable translation of Freud's word *Ruhebett* as *sofa*[13] (we'll return to this in chapter 7), we shall focus for now on the two words highlighted here. They are highlighted because we ought to take seriously the idea that the use of the couch is both *remnant* and *ceremonial*. What that says is that the setup, the *mise en scène*, of the analytic encounter that we now take for granted is *an enactment of a ceremony* rooted in antecedent healing traditions and cultural meanings associated with recumbent posture. And it tells us that for it to even become thinkable to lie down in the presence of another person for the purpose of talking to him or her, there had to be an evolution in attitudes toward the private and the social reflected in the history of recumbence—its social meanings and contexts. Situating the analytic couch within the social history of recumbent posture offers the only way to construct a coherent narrative of the origins of its use in psychoanalysis.

2

Symposion and *Convivium*

The reclining dining posture of the Greek *symposion* and the Roman *convivium*, richly documented in surviving funerary monuments, represented luxury, privilege, leisure, and pleasure to all social classes, not just elites. Far from connoting passivity or submission to authority, recumbent posture was a key indicator of social values. After the decline of reclining dining, recumbent posture was recruited into religious iconography, exemplified by Renaissance depictions of the Nativity of the Virgin Mary.

The common parental admonition to *make your bed* is surely one of the oldest idiomatic expressions in English in continuous use. It likely dates from a time when people pushed straw together on the floor to sleep, and when domesticated animals and their owners were closely quartered. *Bed* is an Old English word whose usage is traceable to the tenth century. The term originally denoted a place for rest dug into the earth; later it meant "the materials upon which people slept."[1] Here etymology reliably indicates human history. Recent archaeological findings indicate that the oldest known beds date to around 70,000 years ago. South African cliff dwellers of that epoch apparently made "mats of branches, sedge, leaves, and rushes to lie on, covering them with laurel leaves to keep away insects."[2] These earliest mats were neither woven nor braided.

With the dawn of the first great civilizations, beds started to change, at least for the wealthy. Most poor people still slept on piles of straw or leaves covered with animal skins (typically from goats or sheep), or perhaps on plain woven mats. Affluent Egyptians, Assyrians, and Persians, however, slept on furniture resembling the modern bed. Archaeologists believe that some of them were quite elegant. They consisted of a wooden frame "strung with a resilient weave of palm leaves, rushes, or leather straps. Furs, tapestries, or blankets were spread on top."[3]

The Greek word κλίνη (*klinē*) meant *that on which one lies*, a bed or a couch; also a funeral bier.[4] This is the word used by Plato in the *Republic* (c. 380 BCE) when Socrates and Glaucon talk about couches and reclining.[5] The *klinē*—whence our words *recline* and *clinic*—was a low, movable bed/couch used for sleeping and eating (see the *klinē* monument in figure 2.1). The frame of the *klinē* was either wood or bronze strung with bands supporting a straw mattress.[6]

In ancient Greece and Rome, it was a sign of status and power to recline at a meal rather than sit. The reclining dining posture indicated privilege, luxury, leisure, and pleasure.[7] This custom probably originated among rulers in the Near East, and was adopted by the Greeks from at least the seventh century BCE. In Greece, it was closely linked with the *symposion*,[8] a drinking party and poetry slam for upper-class males at which truth, beauty, love, and wine itself were the main topics of discussion, and in the Roman Empire with the *convivium*, a banquet with drinking *and* food, typically for men *and* women, ideally with nine or fewer people reclining on three couches arranged in the classic Roman *triclinium* pattern (see figures 2.3 and 2.4).

"In Rome, as earlier in Greece, the practice of reclining to dine spread vertically through society, so that a custom originally aristocratic was imitated by lower social groups," and eventually adopted by ordinary citizens and magistrates, then freedmen and soldiers, all trying to "express their dreams of a privileged life or a happy death."[9] Roman freedmen *and freedwomen*, not just elites, reclined at dinner. Note how in figure 2.5 the woman reclines, her child sits, and the slaves, depicted as childlike, stand—a clear illustration of the hierarchical aspect of posture.

2.1
Funerary stele for Felicita, Roman,
second or third century.

2.2
Greek pottery depicting a symposiast,
c. 480 BCE.

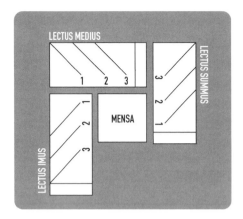

2.3
Diagram of a typical Roman triclinium
(adapted from Dunbabin 2003).

2.4
Depiction of a Roman triclinium.

2.5
Funerary urn depicting a woman,
first century.

Sub-elites (like this woman) liked to depict themselves on their tombstones and funerary monuments as reclining while eating, signifying their changed social status, whereas nobles were more likely to depict their accomplishments.[10] "For ... freedmen or persons of low free birth ... the reclining dining posture ... with its elite connotations, symbolized the status to which they aspired."[11]

In figure 2.6 we again see the classic reclining dining posture, with the dining bowl cupped in the left hand. The image in figure 2.7 is that of a first-century Roman funerary mosaic depicting a married couple banqueting on their dining couches.

2.6
Funerary urn depicting a dining scene,
first century.

2.7
Funerary mosaic, Roman, c. 50–79 CE.

Symposion and *Convivium*

18

Although well-known Renaissance paintings depicting the Last Supper show Jesus and the apostles politely seated around a large table (almost as if there were "invisible place cards spread[ing] a chill through the proceedings";[12] see figures 2.8 and 2.9), according to the Gospels, they ate the Last Supper "lying on their sides,"[13] as earlier representations demonstrate (figures 2.10 and 2.11). A Ravenna mosaic (figure 2.11) is the earliest surviving image of the Last Supper.

Note how different these pre-Renaissance depictions are compared to the more familiar—and much more staid—Last Supper tableaux we've grown accustomed to. A later, seventeenth-century image (figure 2.12) returns us to the recumbence of these earlier depictions of the Last Supper.

Perhaps reflecting a Hellenic influence, middle- and upper-class Romans and Jews reclined to dine for many centuries before and after the time of Christ.[14] Consequently, in Jewish custom, at the traditional Passover *seder* reclining at the meal is a symbol of freedom.[15]

In short, the earliest representations of recumbence connote neither passivity nor submission; rather, they reflect social status, relationships and social hierarchy within social strata, and moral and social values.[16]

Posture has always been an essential component of healing and spiritual traditions.[17] Kneeling to pray is a principal interfaith example. The Greeks built sleep chambers (or sometimes large sleeping halls) in temples of the cult of Asclepius for the express purpose of dream interpretation. The Sanctuary of Asclepius at Epidaurus, dating from the fifth century BCE, is a remarkably well-preserved asclepeion. Many ancient civilizations valued dream interpretation, but the Greek practice of "incubation" (sleeping in the temple in order to be visited by the god while dreaming or, failing that, have a dream that the priest would interpret) antedates Freud's psychoanalytic technique in specifically incorporating supine posture in dream analysis.

2.8
Ugolino da Siena, *Last Supper*,
c. 1325–1330.

2.9
Duccio di Buoninsegna, *Last Supper* from
the Passion Altarpiece, Duomo, Siena,
c. 1278–1318.

2.10
Last Supper, miniature from the Rossano
Gospels (*Codex purpureus Rossanensis*),
parchment manuscript, Greece, sixth century.

2.11
Last Supper, Sant'Apollinare Nuovo,
Ravenna, mosaic, c. 500.

Symposion and *Convivium*

That posture has also long served as an indicator of key social values[18] is illustrated by a brief look at chair portraiture (figures 2.13, 2.14, 2.15, and 2.16). Like the ancient throne (figures 2.13 and 2.14), the medieval chair throne was a symbol of authority (figure 2.15). For a while, chair portraiture was synonymous with authority (figures 2.15 and 2.16), whence our term *chairman*.[19]

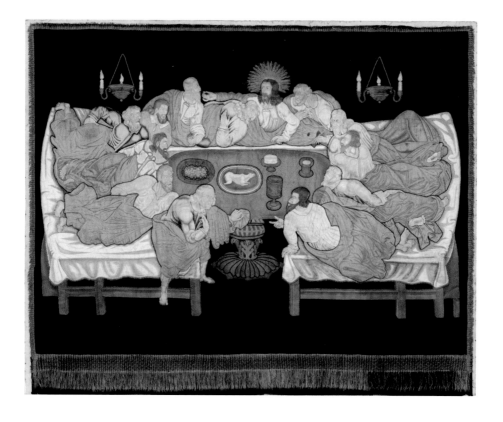

2.12
Last Supper, embroidered altar dossal,
attributed to Edmund Harrison,
England, c. 1633.

2.13
Assyrian ruler or god enthroned,
c. 1500 BCE.

Symposion and *Convivium*

2.14
Relief from the Palace of Ashurbanipal,
Nineveh, showing the Assyrian king
and queen feasting after an important
military victory, c. 645 BCE.

2.15
The French King Philippe IV (1268–1314).

Symposion and *Convivium*

2.16
Studio of Anthonis Mor, *Portrait of
Queen Mary I*, 1554.

Symposion and *Convivium*

For several centuries this was a stable cultural connotation, now transmuted into idiom (*chair*person, *chaired* professorship, or in verb form: to *chair* a committee). In political contexts, both sitting and reclining indicate prestige and authority. So right away we see that Freud's phrase "*a certain ceremonial*" in connection with the use of the couch resonates with a surprisingly long history of ceremonial significance attached to reclining and recumbence.

After the decline of reclining dining, recumbent posture was recruited into religious iconography.

2.17
Pietro Lorenzetti, *Birth of
the Virgin*, 1342.

2.18
Master of the Life of the Virgin,
Birth of the Virgin, c. 1470.

2.19
Vittore Carpaccio, *The Dream of St. Ursula*,
1497–1498.

2.20
Émile-Henri La Porte, *Femme turque allongée*, 1895.

2.21
Divan in Topkapi Palace, Istanbul.

The depiction of the nativity of the Virgin Mary exemplifies this trend (see figures 2.17 and 2.18). Like the baby Jesus, the Virgin Mary would have been born in much more modest circumstances, probably not on a bed at all, since poor people didn't possess beds in those days. As late as the sixteenth century, wood-framed beds were still uncommon enough to be listed among a person's heritable possessions in wills.[20] Yet in numerous Renaissance religious paintings, saints' lives and miracles are dignified by anachronistic placement on contemporaneous beds, as seen in figure 2.19, featuring a historically inaccurate and lavishly appointed bed. This is perhaps because the meaning of private space had evolved, and the Virgin's nativity needed to be seen as part of a recognizable domesticity. These paintings show how the bed had become a marker, an icon of that changed domesticity, in a way that it was not during the life of Jesus. In other words, the bed was becoming a new kind of object, a social signifier in the sense that the Greek and Roman dining couches once were.

If today the bed is associated primarily with sleep and sex, in earlier centuries it was strongly associated with grandeur and privilege, just as the couch was associated with ease and luxury in Greco-Roman culture. Examples of this include the Turkish *divan* (see figures 2.20 and 2.21) and the French *lit de justice*.

The word *divan* was Persian and Arabic before passing into Turkish, and from the Turkish into many European languages. Its mixed etymology bespeaks the measure of authority possessed by those few who could recline in public or official settings. A *divan* originally meant a brochure or account book, but also a tribunal or privy council presided over by the sultan, or a council chamber. And the word also denoted a cushioned bench or raised part of the floor upon which a judge or leader might recline while presiding (figure 2.21).[21]

The *lit de justice* was originally a cushioned dais where the king of France sat for the registration of edicts by royal fiat during sessions of *Parlement.* It evolved from the ornamental beds that began appearing after the thirteenth-century innovation of the bed canopy. The last actual *lit de justice* was convened at Versailles in 1787 during the waning days of the reign of Louis XVI.[22] From sultan to French monarch, the royal and political connotations of recumbent posture and its associated rituals and ceremonies remind us of the changing function and social meaning of reclining and recumbent speech.

3

The Evolution of the Couch and the Rise of the Sofa

Striking changes in eighteenth-century furniture design, epitomized by the rapid popularity of the sofa, reflected and informed changing notions of comfort, domesticity, and intimacy in social settings. As interior decoration began to differentiate itself from architecture, relaxed seating and furniture affording the possibility of intimate conversation came to be regarded as new domestic ideals.

We can trace an evolution in furniture design from the *klinē*, the bed, the bench, the settee (figures 3.1, 3.2, and 3.3), and the daybed or *chaise-longue* (figures 3.4 and 3.5) to the sofa, the invalid chair, the recliner, and the modern upholstered couch.

3.1
Gilded gesso on walnut, covered in eighteenth century silk damask not original to the settee, c. 1730–1735.

3.2
J. Mayhew and W. Ince, settee, 1769.

3.3
Chippendale settee,
1753–1754.

3.4
English daybed, 1690–1710.

3.5
Louis XIV-style beechwood daybed,
Sweden, eighteenth century.

The Evolution of the Couch and the Rise of the Sofa

3.6
Jean-François de Troy, *The Reading from Molière*,
c. 1730.

The English word *couch* derives from the French noun *couche* (dating to the thirteenth century) and the verb *coucher* (twelfth century). One expert contends that the earliest documented English use of *couch* was by King Henry III in 1221,[1] but specific use of the term was probably rare until the sixteenth century. Beds and couches were not clearly distinguished linguistically until approximately that time. Chaucer's fourteenth-century usage, for example, doesn't differentiate them, and even well into the eighteenth century there was considerable ambiguity, as this passage written in 1576 illustrates: "Nature hath not given unto men their ... being, to ... snore in the couche of carelessenesse."[2]

By the seventeenth century, however, rooms and furniture were becoming more specialized and better differentiated. French furniture makers led the way, in part by designing reclining chairs that achieved an almost immediate popularity. Reclining chairs became newly fashionable in early-seventeenth-century France,[3] reflecting a shift in attitudes toward manners and comfort. Under Louis XIV, chairs were mostly part of an architectural aesthetic, made more to be admired than sat in, part of what one author has called the age's "gilded discomfort."[4] Chairs were not upholstered until the seventeenth century. With decreased formality at court under Louis XV, sitting "became a form of relaxation,"[5] marking the differentiation of interior decoration from architecture. Settees began to be placed perpendicular to the wall, rather than aligned against it. Wider, lower chairs permitted conversation (see figure 3.6). New types of *chaises-longues*—the *marquise* and the *duchesse*, for example—were "created exclusively for women's use."[6] These early-eighteenth-century *chaises*, some with adjustable backs, were forerunners of the modern recliner.[7]

Toward the end of the seventeenth century and the beginning of the eighteenth century, French, German, and British craftsmen (but mainly French) began experimenting with new variants on the daybed and the *chaise-longue*, primarily by adding backrests and arms (see figure 3.7).

This gave rise to the *sopha* or *sofa* (figure 3.8), originally a French adaptation of the Arabic *soffah* (cushion). *Sofa* was a word "in use by 1688" and "first mentioned in a [French] dictionary in 1691."[8] It was defined in an eighteenth-century French dictionary as "a 'type of day bed with a back and two arms which has recently come into use in France.'"[9] The sofa and the *ottomane* (figure 3.9), originally a cushioned seat without back or arms, but later just another name for a curvy sofa,[10]

3.7
Print by Dupin after a painting by Leclerc,
Lady in morning *déshabillé*, 1778.

evoked the romanticized Orient (figure 3.10), a popular design theme in eighteenth-century French aristocratic homes and at the royal court (figure 3.11).

Fancy eighteenth-century French furniture fashion bespeaks more than just the whims of wealthy nobles; it offers a lens through which we can perceive changes in cultural ideals of comfort and domesticity, as well as trends in taste and artistic imagination. When it comes to furniture history it would be foolhardy to try to frame sharp distinctions between cause and effect, or to say that the sofa's remarkable popularity was a phenomenon that is best explained by either "top-down" or "bottom-up" kinds of histories. The rise of the sofa was, after all, but a brief moment in an entire (hypothetical) history of conversation, or of comfort, that would ramify in too many directions at once to be comprehended by any single narrative aspiring to coherence. The more the topic is examined, the more one discerns an intricate web of reciprocal influences and contingent causation.[11] Exploring these contingencies and their rich ambiguities is the program of the rest of this book.

3.8
William and Mary-style sofa, c. 1690. The high, vertical back is typical of early sofas. Just as the settee looks only slightly more comfortable than the bench, seventeenth-century sofas look more generously upholstered but only minimally more comfortable than settees.

3.9
Jean-Baptiste I Tilliard, or possibly Jean-Baptiste II Tilliard, *ottomane veilleuse*, carved and gilded beechwood, upholstered in modern red velours de Gênes, c. 1750–1760.

3.10
Jean-Auguste-Dominique Ingres,
Odalisque with Slave, 1839–1840.

3.11
Lit à la turque, c. 1765–1770.

The Evolution of the Couch and the Rise of the Sofa

4

Comfort, Recumbence, Interiority, and Transgression

Early-nineteenth-century portraiture revivified the classic recumbent pose of Greco-Roman funerary monuments. This reclining pose was, and remains, a *leitmotiv* in portraiture ranging from neoclassical divine and mythological subjects to the erotic and the transgressive. The figure of the reclining woman reader, often highly sexualized, offers a clue to understanding what recumbent speech represents: the affirmation in the presence of another of having a mind of one's own.

The meteoric popularity of the sofa heralded a resurrection of the reclining tradition of the Roman *convivium*. In early-nineteenth-century art, this link was quite explicit. David's neoclassical portrait of Madame Récamier (figure 4.1) features the subject clad in a toga-like robe, posing on a couch that can hardly be called plush, her torso supported by bolsters not unlike the cushions that might have been found on the Greco-Roman *klinē*. Canova's contemporaneous sculpture of Paolina Bonaparte Borghese posed as Venus (figure 4.2) similarly invokes the formal elements, including the classic reclining posture, of Roman *klinē* monuments. Canova is perhaps echoing the pose of Giorgione's *Venus Asleep* (figure 4.3). These images reflect the resuscitation of the cultural meanings previously attached to recumbence by the Greeks and Romans.

The reclining pose was—and remains—a *topos* in portraiture ranging from neoclassical divine and mythological subjects (see figure 4.4), to the erotic (figures 4.5 and 4.6) and the transgressive (figure 4.7).

In Maurin's 1892 lithograph (figure 4.7) the physician is depicted as more gluttonous than lascivious, but we see how Asclepius, the God of Health, tempts both the doctor and his beautiful, naked, reclining patient into one sort of transgression or another. Doctoring, ministering to the needs of sufferers, is shown to be a setting pregnant with vice and sin. The patient's recumbent posture and nudity echo the eroticism of the Roman *convivium* (see figures 4.19, 4.20, and 4.21 below), while at the same time indicating how the dangers of exploitation and indiscretion are latent in the healing encounter.[1]

Reclining is a posture midway between lying and sitting. Acceptable and fashionable posture for sitting and reclining changed in tandem with evolving furniture design with a greater emphasis on ease, comfort, and social intimacy.[2]

4.1
Jacques-Louis David,
Madame Récamier,
1805–1806.

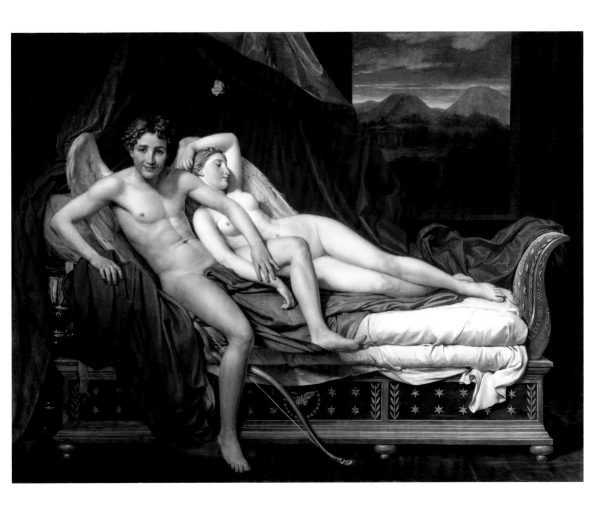

4.2
Antonio Canova, *Paolina Bonaparte Borghese*, 1805–1808.

4.3
Giorgione, *The Sleeping Venus*, 1508–1510.

4.4
Jacques-Louis David, *Cupid and Psyche*, 1817.

4.5
Anonymous, partially nude woman on
a sofa, c. 1900.

4.6
Gustave Le Gray, *Nu féminin allongé sur un
canapé Récamier*, c. 1856.

Comfort, Recumbence, Interiority, and Transgression

The "Récamier" sofa by Duncan Phyfe (figure 4.8) invokes Jacques-Louis David's famous portrait of Madame Récamier (figure 4.1), retaining its neoclassical elegance while adding more cushioning and a backrest for greater comfort. The couch to which the beautiful Madame Récamier lent eponymous fame is perhaps more distinctive in David's rendering, but much less inviting from the standpoint of someone who might actually use it.

4.7
Charles Maurin, *La truffe au médecin et la drogue au client* (Truffles for the doctor, drugs for the patient), lithograph, 1892.

4.8
"Récamier" sofa, attributed to the Workshop of
Duncan Phyfe, c. 1810–1820.

4.9
J. H. Belter, *tête-à-tête*, c. 1850–1860.

56

The so-called *tête-à-tête* (figure 4.9) exemplifies the move toward conversational intimacy in furniture design.

Of particular interest is the *canapé à confidents* (figures 4.10, 4.11, and 4.12), a form explicitly designed for intimate conversation within a social setting. This type of furniture carves out a space for private conversation within a fairly large room like a grand parlor.

These are huge pieces of furniture that obviously could be placed only in a grand room, yet they nevertheless assert the possibility of intimate, private conversation within that rather "public" domestic space. (We'll revisit this furniture form later when we turn to Freud and his couch in chapter 7, but it's not hard to see where we're heading just by looking at how such conversation would have been configured.)

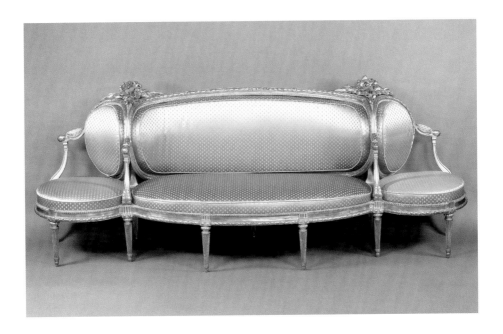

4.10
Claude I Sené, *canapé à confidents*, carved
and gilded beechwood upholstered in
modern blue dotted silk, c. 1775–1780.

4.11
Jean-Baptiste Lebas, Louis XV *canapé à confidents*, c. 1750.

4.12
Napoléon III carved giltwood *canapé à confidents*, c. 1850.

Lest we assume that changing notions of privacy and comfort follow routinely or automatically upon technological innovation, note that invention and revolution in furniture design in the eighteenth century was *not* matched by significant changes in how a home was heated or lit, nor by significant improvements in home water supply or sanitation. These came much later. Well after stoves were shown to heat a house more efficiently, more economically (with respect to fuel costs), and more comfortably (in terms of smokiness) than fireplaces, people of all socioeconomic classes were slow to adopt them.[3] Why did people resist change? There is no simple or singular answer, but the question is worth asking. Perhaps a hearth was an important part of what made a house feel like a home. In any case, it is also worth noting that systems of central heating and ventilation came first not to rich people's domiciles, but to large institutions like prisons and poorhouses.[4] The same is true of indoor plumbing and the modern flush toilet: they were slow in becoming a standard design feature even in wealthy private homes. Only the most luxurious eighteenth-century homes had bathrooms or private toilets.[5] Commode seats and chamber pots were used in the open space of a room. Bathroom privacy and the use of water supplied by indoor plumbing largely awaited the last quarter of the nineteenth century[6]—in other words, long after these eighteenth-century changes in furniture design.

Even in the second half of the eighteenth century, cleanliness was still more a matter of clothing, powder, and perfume than of bathing; the term *toilette* did not presuppose the use of water.[7] The point here again is that eighteenth-century changes in furniture design, and in notions of domestic interiority and comfort, long preceded technological changes in domestic life with respect to heating, lighting, and plumbing.

These eighteenth-century changes in furniture design both resulted from and informed changes in clothing, manners, and deportment. This is especially (but not exclusively) true of women's clothing. Recumbence, or even relaxed seating, was out of the question for tightly corseted women, or women wearing dresses with bustles.

Here (in figure 4.13), for example, we see the wife of King Louis XV, queen consort of France from 1725 until her death in 1768, in a dress that no woman could possibly put on or take off by herself. The wasp-waist bodice stiffens and constrains her body; reclining in this dress would have been impossible.[8]

The same is true of the clothing for both husband and wife in figure 4.14, but note also how the entire domestic surround is stiff and formal, in contrast to the entirely different garb, posture, and deportment of the women depicted in figures 4.15, 4.16, 4.17, 4.25, 4.26, 4.27, 4.28, and 4.29. Note the stark contrast between the images of domesticity depicted in figures 4.14 and 4.15.

As newer, less restrictive corsets replaced the bustle, and as dresses with built-in stays of ivory and bone were replaced by looser-fitting dresses (see figures 4.15, 4.16, and 4.17) worn with undergarments (at first with, then without, stays), it became possible even for fashion-conscious women to read and converse in relaxed and intimate postures that the new furniture styles encouraged and responded to.

4.13
Jean-Louis Toqué, *Queen Maria Leszczyńska*, 1740.

4.14
Arthur Devis, *Mr & Mrs Richard
Bull*, 1747.

4.15
Pierre-Paul Prud'hon,
The Schimmelpenninck Family,
1801–1802.

Comfort, Recumbence, Interiority, and Transgression

4.16
Gottlieb Schick, *Frau von Cotta*, 1802.

4.17
Franz Xaver Winterhalter, *Leonilla
Bariatinskaia, Princess of Sayn Wittgenstein
Sayn*, 1843.

4.18
"The *spécialité* corset is a dream of
comfort," 1901 advertisement.

February 2nd, 1901 *THE LADIES' FIELD*

THE "SPÉCIALITÉ CORSET"

IS A DREAM OF COMFORT.

Regd. Design No. 2517.

THE **"SPÉCIALITÉ CORSET"** is manufactured under scientific supervision, the cut and make being perfect. Each bone is placed in the position requiring support, without impeding or checking the proper exercise of the muscles, allowing perfect freedom of action to the whole frame; all these advantages are obtained, with an additional elegance of form, as the Illustration will show.

The "Spécialité Corset" is made of the best materials, and fitted throughout with **REAL WHALEBONE** (busks and side-steels excepted), best sewing and perfect finish. The quality of the "Spécialité Corset" will be found 25 per cent. better, at the price, than any other Corset offered to the public.

☞ **CAUTION.** The **"SPÉCIALITÉ CORSET"** is made only for us, and cannot be had Wholesale or Retail except through

THE NEW STRAIGHT-FRONTED **"SPÉCIALITÉ CORSET"** (*as illustration*), in White Coutille and real Whalebone, price **27/6**; in Black Coutille, unlined, **29/6**.
THE **"SPÉCIALITÉ CORSET."**—TYPE **1A**.—Long waist, in Black Italian Cloth and Real Whalebone, **19/6** complete; in Black Satin, **27/6**.
  TYPE **1B**.—Extra long waist, in Black Italian Cloth and Real Whalebone, **21/-** complete; in Black Satin, **29/6**.
  TYPE **1C**.—Long waist, cut longer below the waist, and extra fully boned to give greater support to stout figures, in Black or White, **25/-** complete.
  TYPE **2D**.—Long waist, in White Coutille and Real Whalebone, **18/6**.
  TYPE **2E**.—Extra long waist, **21/-** complete.
  TYPE **2F**.—Extra long waist, and cut longer below the waist to suit ladies requiring a high and deep make. In White Coutille and Real Whalebone, **25/-** complete.
  TYPE **3G**.—Medium waist, in White Coutille and Real Whalebone, **16/6**.

Comfort, Recumbence, Interiority, and Transgression

The corset advertised in figure 4.18 illustrates the trend toward less restrictive undergarments. Softer, more pliable corsets and corsets designed to be worn higher up on the body allowed at least some degree of freer movement, and meant that reclining on a sofa was possible. These developments in fashion were not linear; the notion that women's attire should be less restrictive waxed and waned throughout the nineteenth century, and was not firmly established until the twentieth.[9]

There is something undeniably erotic and transgressive about recumbent posture (see figures 4.19, 4.20, and 4.21); to lose sight of this is to ignore not only the rich iconography of recumbence, but also its repudiation for about a thousand years.

4.19
Banqueting couple with
a slave, Herculaneum
dining mural (fresco),
Roman, c. 50–79 CE.

4.20
Pompeii dining panel,
first century.

4.21
Triclinium scene, fresco,
Pompeii, first century.

In terms of mores, reclining in social settings was lost in the West from the end of the Roman Empire until the dawn of the eighteenth century and the rise of the sofa (see figures 4.22, 4.23, and 4.24).

Throughout the eighteenth and nineteenth centuries, the sofa was the favored site for the depiction by artists of the way manners and fashion were changing. The languorous poses seen in figures 4.25–4.31 represent a recrudescence of the reclining traditions of the Greek *symposion* and the Roman *convivium*. Newly emerging ideals of comfort were becoming inseparable from notions of social intimacy. Recumbent speech, long suppressed since the decline of the Greco-Roman tradition of reclining dining, was now renascent in the West, revolutionizing the appearance and practice of intimate conversation. These are among the changes that provided the cultural conditions necessary for the eventual emergence of psychotherapy in general, and psychoanalysis in particular.

4.22
Édouard Manet, *Olympia*, 1863.

4.23
Photograph attributed to Wilhelm von Plüschow, Italy, c. 1900. Compared to its female counterpart, the image of the reclining male nude is less frequently encountered in nineteenth-century couch portraiture, though by no means absent. Compare this décor, with its kilims and tapestry or rug hanging above the couch, to the images of Freud's couch in figures 7.1, 8.5, and 8.7.

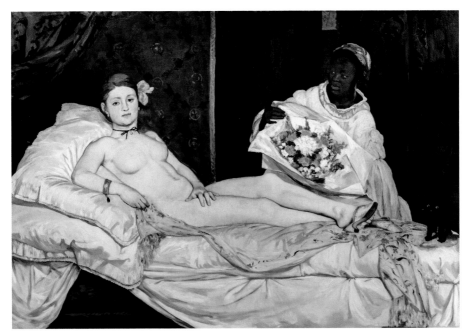

Comfort, Recumbence, Interiority, and Transgression

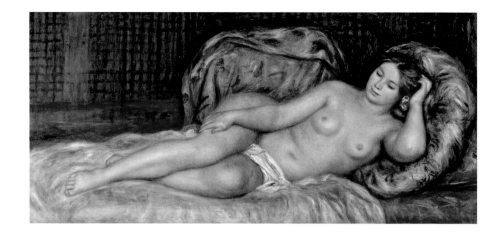

4.24
Auguste Renoir, *Large Nude*, 1907.

4.25
Jean-François de Troy, *La déclaration d'amour*
(The Declaration of Love), 1724.

Comfort, Recumbence, Interiority, and Transgression

4.26
Konstantin Somov, *A Sleeping Woman*, 1909.

4.27
Domingo Marques, *A Moment of Repose*,
c. 1900.

4.28
John Singer Sargent, *Nonchaloir
(Repose)*, 1911.

4.29
Ramon Casas i Carbó, *After the Ball*, 1895.

Comfort, Recumbence, Interiority, and Transgression

In figures 4.30 and 4.31, respectively, we see two Victorian portraits from not long before and shortly after Freud began using the couch.

In François Boucher's *The Toilette of Venus* (figure 4.32), the portrayal of Venus on a sofa is, iconographically speaking, the Enlightenment analogue of the Renaissance nativity scenes in which the Virgin Mary is born on a bed. The goddess of beauty deserves—and here visually discourses upon—comfort, ease, and luxury. Boucher's 1751 painting reflects the very latest in high-end furniture fashion, and in so doing it limns a new asymptote on the aspirational axis of manners and deportment. It tells *all* viewers—not just rich ones—what they ought to be aiming for and dreaming of, domestically as well as sexually.

4.30
Anonymous, napping woman, c. 1865.

4.31
W. G. Levison, *Rosalie Kelsey*, c. 1890.

Comfort, Recumbence, Interiority, and Transgression

Compare this to his 1756 portrait of the Marquise de Pompadour (figure 4.33): besides being a great beauty, quite at ease with herself, this woman is a reader and a writer. She holds a well-thumbed book, her fingers perhaps marking favorite passages, and next to her a small writing table stands at the ready, with sealing wax and a quill poised in the inkwell of an open drawer.[10] The large tome under her writing table is a volume of Diderot's *Encyclopédie.* Her reclining posture is calculated to show off her fancy shoes and the amazing quantity of expensive fabric involved in the composition of her dress, but also her ease with the identity of a woman of intellect.

4.32
François Boucher, *The Toilette of Venus*, 1751.

4.33
François Boucher, *Madame de Pompadour*, 1756.

The figure of the female intellectual was not unprecedented in Madame de Pompadour's day, but neither was it widely acceptable. Historically, the idealization of women and feminine beauty has always been paired with hatred of and cruelty toward women. The rise of Mariolatry (worship of the Virgin Mary) in the twelfth and thirteenth centuries corresponded with a period of intense misogyny. Behind the literary and artistic admiration, celebration, and idealization of feminine beauty looms the specter of the European witchcraft craze. The persecution of women as witches was very much a Renaissance phenomenon; witchcraft trials and executions, begun in the Middle Ages, peaked in the seventeenth century, the so-called Age of Reason.[11] Artistic images of recumbent female nudes are backlit, so to speak, by this dark history. Misogyny in contemporary Western culture is covertly expressed in the adoration of female beauty as well as in the obsessive striving for its attainment and perfection. The male gaze, as reflected in the examples of female portraiture seen throughout this book, conveys the twin poles of this ambivalence toward women, informed as it has always been by men's fears of and concerns about female sexuality.

The European witchcraft craze was, among other things, a horrific concretization of these fears. But men's fantasies about female sexuality also received cultural expression in many other areas of morality and manners. The notion that female sexuality is somehow poorly contained or out of control has a long secular (as well as theological) history, and we see how that very traditional idea is embedded, so to speak, with the view that novels present women readers with the dangers of corruption and immorality in the form of unbridled eroticism (see figures 4.34 and 4.35).[12]

Note how in figure 4.34 the reader's left hand has slipped suspiciously under her skirts. And note how in figure 4.35, an image from about a century later, the Devil is slipping her one ruinous novel after another. Here the woman reader is depicted as wanton, wayward, and undone by her interest in and enjoyment of the fantasy world of fiction.

The sexualization of the woman reader (evident in images like the paintings in figures 4.34 and 4.35) defends against an even greater danger—namely, the threat represented by a woman having her own unmediated experience of literature, her own private thoughts, her own mind (see figure 4.36).

4.34
Pierre-Antoine Baudouin, *The Reader*, 1760.

4.35
Antoine Wiertz, *La liseuse
de romans* (The Reader of
Novels), 1853.

4.36
Jean-Honoré Fragonard,
La liseuse (Young girl
reading), 1776.

This is what was truly transgressive—or at least, potentially subversive or nonconformist—about psychoanalysis at its inception, and this is part of what recumbent speech represents: the affirmation in the presence of another of having a mind of one's own.

Here is another recumbent woman reader (figure 4.37), *avant la lettre*, so to speak, well before the invention of the printing press, and yet another more recent one (figure 4.38).

4.37
Tomb of Eleanor of Aquitaine,
c. 1210, detail.

4.38
Pablo Picasso, *Femme couchée lisant*
(Reclining Woman Reading), 1960.

Comfort, Recumbence, Interiority, and Transgression

5

The Medicalization of Comfort

The nineteenth century ushered in a dramatic rise in the production of portable and invalid furniture. Swelling numbers of war casualties, greater wealth among the bourgeoisie—with a concomitant need for furniture to rent or purchase on seaside excursions—and a growing number of patients with chronic medical illnesses—primarily tuberculosis—all gave impetus to innovation, and the proliferation of recliners and adjustable *chaises-longues.* The portable and cleansable recliner of the TB sanatorium was a medical icon throughout the West, strongly influencing subsequent modernist design style and medical practice.

Looking at the piece of furniture the French called a *duchesse* (or sometimes a *duchesse brisée* if the chair portion and foot portion were separated, as in figure 5.1), we find a design form that can be tracked through the next three images: Boucher's portrait of his wife (figure 5.2), Lewis Carroll's portrait of Xie Kitchin (figure 5.3), and the painting by Balthus entitled *The Golden Years* (figure 5.4).

These three images span two hundred years, chronologically encasing Sigmund Freud's lifetime (1856–1939).

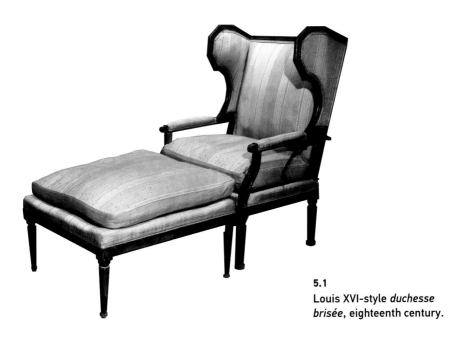

5.1
Louis XVI-style *duchesse brisée*, eighteenth century.

The Medicalization of Comfort

5.3
Lewis Carroll, *Portrait of Xie Kitchin*, 1873.

5.4
Balthus (Balthasar Klossowski),
The Golden Years, c. 1945.

The Medicalization of Comfort

5.5
Saint-Georges, *veilleuse*,
c. 1750.

5.6
Henri Rousseau, *The Dream*, 1910.

Looking as well at the furniture (called a *veilleuse*) in the two images in figures 5.5 and 5.6, and the recumbent pose in the images in figures 5.7–5.11, we can see in juxtaposing them that there is a *leitmotiv* in the iconography of recumbence in the West that retains all the original ambiguities of the reclining dining posture of the Greek *symposion* and the Roman *convivium*, in the sense that these settings stake out the intersection of ease, comfort, luxury, and eroticism. With the medicalization of comfort, recumbent posture became part of the technology of healing.

5.7
Klinē monument, dedicated by Flavius Agricola, second century. Compare figure 4.2 (reproduced at right).

5.8
Jean-Baptiste-Camille Corot, *Bacchante
by the Sea*, 1865.

5.9
E. J. Bellocq, untitled nude from the
Storyville Portraits series, c. 1920.

5.10
Titian, *Venus of Urbino* (before 1538).

5.11
Émile Bernard, *Madeleine au Bois d'Amour*, 1888.

5.12
American Civil War injured.

Beginning in the early nineteenth century, there was a dramatic increase in the production of portable and invalid furniture.[1] Several factors gave impetus to this: (1) warfare (consider, for example, the Napoleonic, Crimean, and American Civil Wars), which created swelling numbers of casualties and invalids (see figure 5.12); (2) greater wealth among the bourgeoisie, leading to the growing pursuit of travel, leisure, and relaxation, with a concomitant need for furniture to bring, rent, or purchase on seaside excursions (see figures 5.13 and 5.14);[2] and (3) a large increase in the number of patients with chronic medical illnesses, primarily tuberculosis, but also syphilis, malaria, gout, and other illnesses.[3]

HOME COMFORTS
from the catalogue of
John Carter, 1897.

5.13 and 5.14
"The Triclinium," open and closed positions,
1897 furniture catalog.

The Medicalization of Comfort

TB was the leading cause of death among European and American adults in the eighteenth and nineteenth centuries. Robert Koch (1843–1910) identified the tubercle bacillus (*Mycobacterium tuberculosis*) in 1882, but from the early nineteenth century until the 1950s,[4] the primary treatment for TB, originated by German physicians, was the open-air rest cure known as the *Luft-Liegekur*[5] (see figures 5.16, 5.17, 5.18, and 5.21). So for more than a hundred years, certainly including Freud's entire lifetime, this was *the* treatment for TB.

Both furniture makers and physicians sought numerous patents for improvements and variations upon the adjustable *chaise-longue*.[6] The *Schlafsofa* (sleep sofa or recliner couch), described in detail in Thomas Mann's *The Magic Mountain* (1928), was a fixture of *Liegehallen* (rest halls) in sanatoria throughout Europe and the U.S., and a medical icon throughout the West (see figures 5.20 and 5.21).[7]

As a physician who trained during a period when TB was a leading medical scourge, Freud would have been steeped in the culture of the sanatorium and the *Luft-Liegekur*.

5.15
TB testing poster, WPA, Chicago, 1939.

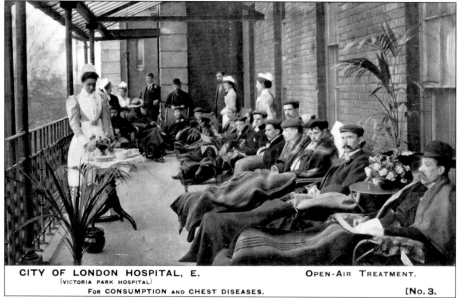

CITY OF LONDON HOSPITAL, E.
(VICTORIA PARK HOSPITAL)
For CONSUMPTION and CHEST DISEASES.

OPEN-AIR TREATMENT.

[No. 3.

5.16
The open-air cure originally known as
the *Luft-Liegekur*, City of London Hospital,
c. 1890.

5.17
Children at a convalescent home in the
Vosges, c. 1930.

5.18
Another open-air cure photo, c. 1890.

Sanatorium de BEL-AIR — Cure d'été

FIG. 3.—THE BARWISE REST-CHAIR.

This novel form of wheel hammock is manufactured by the Smith and Cartwright Bedstead Company, Limited, Hertford Street, Balsall Heath, Birmingham, and is in use at the Derbyshire Sanatorium.

5.19
The Barwise Rest-chair, a wheeled hammock used at the Derbyshire Sanatorium for tuberculosis patients, c. 1916 (from Barwise 1916, cited by Campbell 1999).

5.20
Wakefield Rattan Company advertisement, 1879.

5.21
Liegehalle photo, 1916.

A VERY COMFORTABLE RECLINING CHAIR.

As one furniture historian observes, "the nineteenth-century invalid chair was neither chair nor couch, but a hybrid that could fluctuate between the two [see figures 5.22 and 5.23]. The United States took the lead in the development of this type of chair starting in the 1830s and increasing at a great pace after the 1850s,"[8] resulting in the production of specialized forms for barbers, surgeons, dentists, and gynecologists (figure 5.24).[9]

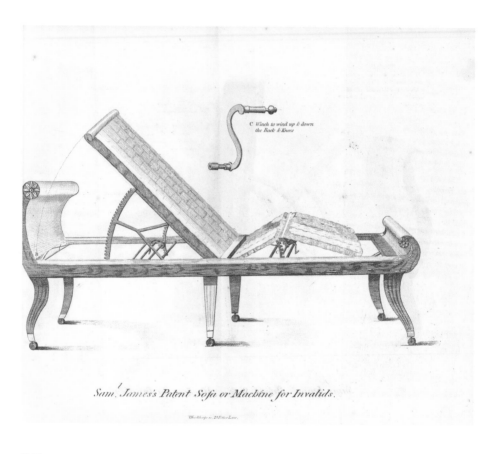

Saml. James's Patent Sofa or Machine for Invalids.

5.22
Saml. James's Patent Sofa or
Machine for Invalids,
early nineteenth century.

5.23
Pocock's Reclining Patent Chair,
from *Ackermann's Repository of Arts*,
print, 1813.

5.24
Gynecologic chair, 1878.

The Medicalization of Comfort

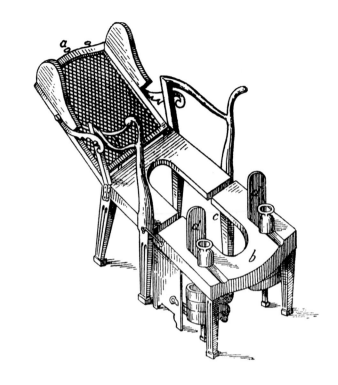

5.25
Obstetric chair, 1891.

5.26
Delivery table, 1887.

A.D. 1852. October 30. Nº 578.

KIRBY'S Provisional Specification.

FIG.1.

5.27
Kirby's Adjusting Couch for Medical
and Surgical Purposes, 1852.

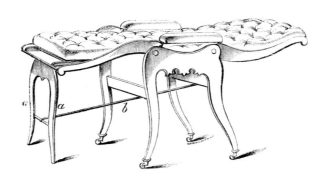

5.28
Upholstered exam table,
mid-nineteenth century.

The Medicalization of Comfort

5.29
Adjusting exam couch, nineteenth century.

5.30
Poster art from Freud's Vienna, in
Österreichische Plakatkunst, 1914. Note
the striking similarity between the recliner
of the nineteenth-century TB sanatorium
(as seen, for example, in figure 5.19)
and that of the early-twentieth-century
modernist style.

5.31 (opposite)
Charlotte Perriand on the B306
chaise-longue designed by Perriand and
Le Corbusier.

"The mechanized forms of the chaise longue, the sofa, the couch and the fauteuil, developed and refined during the second half of the nineteenth century (in part in response to the demands of nursing and surgery), made it possible to adjust to as many gradations as possible between sitting and lying."[10] Variants include the modern medical examination table, a fixture in doctors' offices for well over a century (see figures 5.25–5.29). Production of specialized medical recliners peaked in the U.S. in the 1870s and 1880s.[11]

The *Schlafsofa* of the TB sanatorium had to be cheap, portable, and easily sanitized—all of which meant that it also had to be un-upholstered. These features lent themselves to the subsequent elaboration of the *Schlafsofa* into a sleek interior design element, reflecting the fusion of medical science, modern design, and popular notions of health and well-being (see figures 5.30–5.36).

The early-twentieth-century modernist architectural style was pioneered largely by men and women who had designed (or drew upon designs of) recliners for TB sanatoria before turning them into upscale domestic furnishings.[12]

As fresh air, sunning, and relaxing became healthy pursuits (see figures 5.33, 5.34, 5.35 and 5.36), the Greco-Roman dining couch was (once again) reborn as the key accoutrement and symbol of living well.

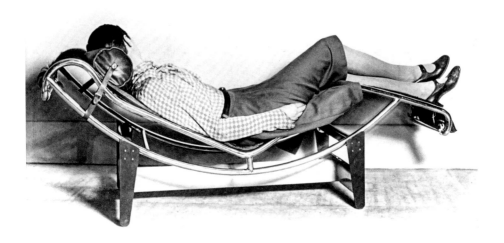

5.32 (left)
Mies van der Rohe,
Barcelona Chaise, 1930.

5.33
"Roman divan" couches
from a 1902 Sears
Roebuck catalog.

5.34
"Le Surrepos,"
advertisement, 1922.

5.35 (left)
Thonet bentwood
reclining rocker,
Austria, c. 1870.

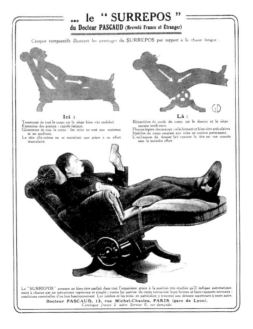

The Medicalization of Comfort

5.36
Samuel Clemens (Mark Twain), inveterate
napper and relaxer, c. 1890.

6

Recumbent Posture in Nineteenth-Century Psychiatry and Therapeutics

The major psychiatric treatments of the nineteenth century—hypnosis, hydrotherapy, cutaneous electrotherapy, phototherapy, diet and rest cures—all sought to import ideals of comfort and healthy relaxation derived from the long dominance of the open-air rest cure of the TB sanatoria. All of these treatment modalities promoted an association in the minds of practitioners and patients alike between recumbence and cure. Freud trained in and was shaped by this medical culture before profoundly shaping it himself.

Nineteenth-century alienists,[1] asylum keepers, psychologists, and university-based psychiatrists employed a wide variety of somatic and suggestive therapies. These included hypnosis, hydrotherapy, cutaneous electrotherapy, phototherapy, diet and rest cures, massage, and, with the introduction of chemically prepared (as opposed to plant-derived) sedatives such as chloral hydrate in 1869, some early efforts at modern psychopharmacology. Since these treatment modalities (with the exception of psychopharmacology) usually required recumbent posture, it seems reasonable to infer that their popularity promoted an association in the minds of patients and practitioners alike between recumbence and cure. Here, too, it would be glib to speak simply of submission to medical authority when many of these treatments sought to import ideals of domestic ease and comfort into the psychiatric setting.

Trance states (see figure 6.1) were initially construed to be a form of "neuro-hypnotism" or "nervous sleep,"[2] so it made sense for practitioners to have furniture suitable for reclining, sleeping, swooning, or becoming entranced while recumbent.[3] During his 1885–1886 sojourn in Paris at the Salpêtrière Hospital, Freud learned about hypnosis in the treatment of hysteria from the world-famous neurologist Jean-Martin Charcot. Upon his return to Vienna, as he embarked upon the private practice of clinical neurology specializing in the treatment of nervous and mental disorders, Freud settled into a ten-year dalliance with hypnosis.

At the height of Charcot's rivalry with Hippolyte Bernheim in the 1880s and 1890s over suggestibility and the nature of hypnosis, Freud translated both men's work into German and wrote prefaces to the three volumes of their writings he translated.[4] Bernheim and his followers in the Nancy school of hypnotists, including August Forel, Leopold Löwenfeld, Oskar Vogt, and Otto Wetterstrand, emphasized the need for a calm, quiet environment for their treatments and encouraged patients to fall asleep during hypnotic sessions.[5] The private practice of German hypnosis doctors, among them some of the leading contributors to the *Zeitschrift für Hypnotismus*, was dominated by this approach.[6] This development coincided with the rise of office-based private practice in Germany and Austria, and the emergence of the tradition of the reserved office hour.[7] Freud's early practice of hypnosis was modeled upon the Nancy school's emphasis on recumbence and sleep.

Along with hypnosis, Freud's early forays into psychological medicine included the practice of massage and cutaneous electrotherapy, including the use of the faradic brush (see figures 6.2, 6.3, 6.4, and 6.5).

In his *Autobiographical Study*, Freud writes candidly that at the start of his clinical career, "My therapeutic arsenal contained only two weapons, electrotherapy and hypnotism, for prescribing a visit to a hydropathic establishment after a single consultation was an inadequate source of income."[8] He adds that his knowledge of electrotherapy was derived from Wilhelm Erb's *Handbuch der Electrotherapie* of 1882 (see figure 6.6), a work cited three times in the *Standard Edition of the Complete Psychological Works of Sigmund Freud*. In an 1888 encyclopedia article on "Hysteria," Freud enthusiastically endorses the Weir Mitchell rest cure, consisting, as he describes it, of "isolation in absolute quiet with a systematic application of massage and general faradizations."[9]

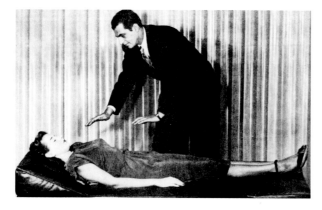

6.1
Hypnotic subject on a couch, c. 1941.

6.2
Faradic brush for cutaneous electrotherapy, nineteenth century.

6.3
Dr. Scott's Electric Hair and Flesh Brush (engraving), English, advertisement, 1882. The brush's inscription declares that "The germ of all life is electricity."

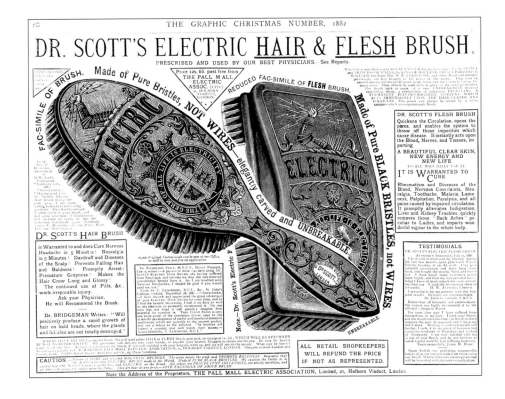

118

FIG. 79.—Sponge Clasps (Kidder).

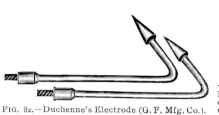

FIG. 82.—Duchenne's Electrode (G. F. Mfg. Co.).

FIG. 84.—Rockwell's Brass Ball Electrode for General Faradization (Kidder).

FIG. 86.—Hand Sponge Electrode (Van Houten & Ten Broeck).

FIG. 83.—Folding Foot Plate (McIntosh).

FIG. 85.—Stationary Electrode.

FIG. 87.—Sponge Electrode with Handle for use under the Clothing (Van Houten & Ten Broeck).

6.4
Hand sponge electrode, from an 1896 book on electrotherapy.

FIG. 93.—Metallic Brush
(G. F. Mfg. Co.).

FIG. 94.—Wheel Electrode for
Muscular Faradization (Mc-
Intosh).

6.5
Metallic brush and wheel electrode for
muscular faradization, from the same
book (Rockwell, 1896).

Recumbent Posture in Nineteenth-Century Psychiatry and Therapeutics

Hydrotherapy (see figures 6.7 and 6.8) was a traditional, asylum-based nineteenth-century treatment for hysteria and other mental maladies that Freud, like all practitioners of his generation, was well aware of.

Phototherapy, sometimes combined with hydrotherapy, was a somewhat more cutting-edge treatment modality emerging in the latter decades of the nineteenth century. Phototherapy, with or without hydrotherapy, was considered an indicated treatment for hysteria, epilepsy, neurasthenia, migraine, melancholia, mania, GPI (General Paresis of the Insane, or neurosyphilis), insomnia, and a wide variety of other psychiatric, neurological, and general medical disorders (see figures 6.9, 6.10, and 6.11).[10]

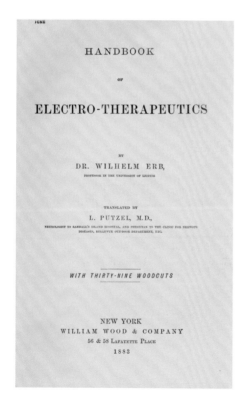

6.6
Title page of the 1883 English translation of Wilhelm Erb's *Handbuch der Electrotherapie* (1882), a book cited repeatedly by Freud.

6.7 and 6.8
Two images from Trall's *Hydropathic Encyclopedia* (1853). Notice how similar the furniture in these images is to the *veilleuse* in figures 5.5 and 5.6.

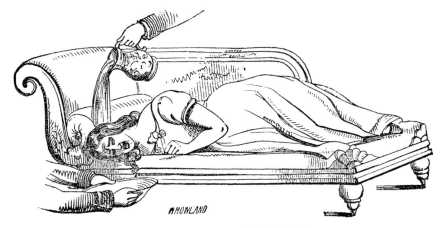

TREATMENT OF HYSTERIA.

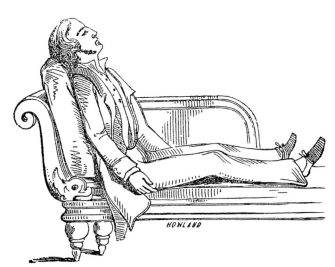

POSITION IN APOPLEXY.

Recumbent Posture in Nineteenth-Century Psychiatry and Therapeutics

Light Therapeutics

A Practical Manual of Phototherapy for the
Student and the Practitioner

With Special Reference to the Incandescent
Electric-Light Bath

By J. H. KELLOGG, M. D.

Author of "Rational Hydrotherapy," "The Art of Massage," etc. Member of the
British Gynæcological Society, the International Periodical Congress of Gynæ-
cology and Obstetrics, American and British Associations for the Ad-
vancement of Science, the Société d'Hygiène of France, American
Society of Microscopists, American Climatological Society,
American Medical Association, Michigan State
Medical Society, Superintendent of the
Battle Creek (Mich.) Sanitarium

BATTLE CREEK, MICH.
THE GOOD HEALTH PUBLISHING CO.
Publishers of Therapeutic Manuals
1910

6.9
Title page of J. H. Kellogg's *Light Therapeutics* (1910). Figures 6.10 and 6.11 are also from this book.

6.10
Phototherapy in the first decade of the twentieth century.

6.11
Illustration of recumbent posture in the "modern" hydrotherapy of Freud's day.

Fig. 28. Arc Light to the shoulder. See page 98.

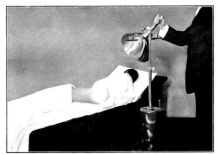

Fig. 29. Arc Light to the hip and thigh. See page 98.

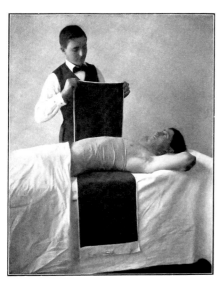

Fig. 55. The Wet Girdle. See page 135.

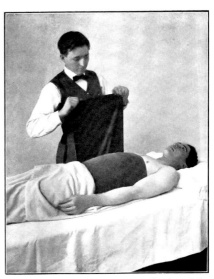

Fig. 56. The Wet Girdle—The application of the outer covering. See page 135.

6.12
Private patient's room, The New York
Hospital, illustration by W. P. Snyder,
Harper's Magazine, 1878.

Thus, the use of recumbent posture in psychoanalysis evolved in part from these traditions of sanatorium- and asylum-based somatic therapies as well as from the broader cultural backdrop of changing notions of comfort and interiority, eventuating in what I have called the medicalization of comfort (chapter 5). Figure 6.12 nicely illustrates this point. In this image, published in *Harper's Magazine* in 1878, the hospitalized patient is seen resting comfortably in a recliner that closely resembles the standard *chaise-longue* of the TB sanatorium (see figures 5.16–5.21 above). His concerned family members attend him in seated comfort, one of them in what appears to be a rocking chair. The scene is one of institutionalized domesticity. At least for the private patient, some trappings of the comforts of home accompany him during his hospital stay. His recumbent posture signifies how, by the time Freud began to develop his ideas about the optimal treatment setting for psychoanalysis, notions of healing and comfort had thoroughly melded.

Freud's Couch

Freud's couch antedates psychoanalysis in that he began using it in the 1880s while he was still practicing hypnosis, massage, and electrotherapy, and just beginning to become interested in the free association method. As he gradually shed hypnotic, electrotherapeutic, and other more directive approaches, he retained the use of recumbent posture, and this soon became a distinctive feature of his psychotherapeutic technique. Freud's couch and his surrounding antiquities collection convey his ties to romanticism as well as to the fixtures of earlier asylum-based and medical treatments.

Sigmund Freud's couch (figure 7.1) is both *Ruhebett* (daybed) and Turkish divan, carrying the twin identities of sanatorium and asylum fixture on the one hand, and romantic symbol on the other.

7.1
Freud's couch at the Freud Museum
in London.

Freud's couch also antedates psychoanalysis in the sense that he obtained it and began using it clinically during the years when he was steeped in the practice of hypnosis (which in the1880s he often combined with massage and cutaneous electrotherapy), the cathartic method pioneered by Breuer and Freud,[1] and what he called "the pressure technique." Freud would place his hand upon the forehead of his recumbent patient and demand the production of a train of free associations.

Freud soon realized that his pressure technique was clumsy and overbearing, but it marked an important step in his theorization of the dynamic unconscious, then underway. The pressure technique reflected Freud's deepening commitment to psychic determinism, the notion that psychic elements are linked in a causal chain and that mental phenomena are always meaningful, never accidental or arbitrary.[2] Pressuring patients to come up with the associative links Freud wanted, the ones he felt sure would lead to the uncovering of crucial causal links buried in the unconscious, was not at all a good technique, and Freud soon discarded it.

MANKOFF

"Now, we can get all those repressed memories the easy way or the hard way."

7.2
A 2008 *New Yorker* cartoon that could be viewed as a satiric depiction of Freud's "pressure technique."

In retrospect, it is easily mocked. But it behooves us to stop and think why Freud would have tried it in the first place. He hadn't yet come to his later appreciation of the crucial significance of the interplay of free association and the forces that oppose self-revelation and self-knowledge; the failure of the pressure technique was an important part of his journey. The same is true of his prolonged dabbling in the authoritarian method of hypnotic suggestion. Freud stated candidly that he wasn't very good at hypnotic treatment, and that his inability to hypnotize all patients frustrated and embarrassed him.[3] But the problems of varying and capricious hypnotizability and the continuum of human suggestibility also forced him to think more carefully about resistance and repression. Respecting these barriers to cure was another step on the path toward his eventual elaboration of a more fully theorized dynamic unconscious. From the point of view of therapeutic technique, Freud's use of the couch was the one constant feature in his journey from hypnosis and suggestion to psychoanalysis.

The independent Freud historian Peter Swales sees Freud's patient Anna von Lieben (1847–1900) as a major influence in his adoption of the use of the couch. Freud treated her in the late 1880s and early 1890s; she is the "Frau Cäcilie M" of the *Studies on Hysteria* published in 1895 by Breuer and Freud. Swales describes her as "a woman who spent much of her life, and probably all of her treatment, reclining on a *chaise-longue*."[4] Freud administered morphine and massage in addition to hypnosis (the latter in conjunction with his pressure technique).[5] In July 1889, during his treatment of her, she accompanied him on a visit to the leading French hypnotists Liébeault and Bernheim in Nancy. During their visit, he made daily calls on her in her hotel,[6] where he presumably ministered to her in her bed or on a daybed or sofa in her hotel sitting room.

Swales also notes that in May 1889 Freud was treating "Frau Emmy von N" (also of the *Studies*) "on a sofa" (*auf dem Diwan*), and instructs Miss Lucy R to "lie down."[7] By 1891 or 1892, he had adopted the regular use of the couch,[8] perhaps following his move in September 1891 to the more spacious home and consulting rooms of Berggasse 19.

But in all likelihood Freud had been using one sort of *chaise-longue* or another since opening his private practice in 1886, initially modeling his hypnotic and suggestive treatments on the practice of Liébeault and Bernheim (see chapter 6).[9] Indeed, in 1883 he had visited an exhibition in Vienna of model domestic interiors showcasing the newly available electric lighting (see figures 7.4 and 7.5).

7.3
Freud in 1891, the year he moved to
Berggasse 19.

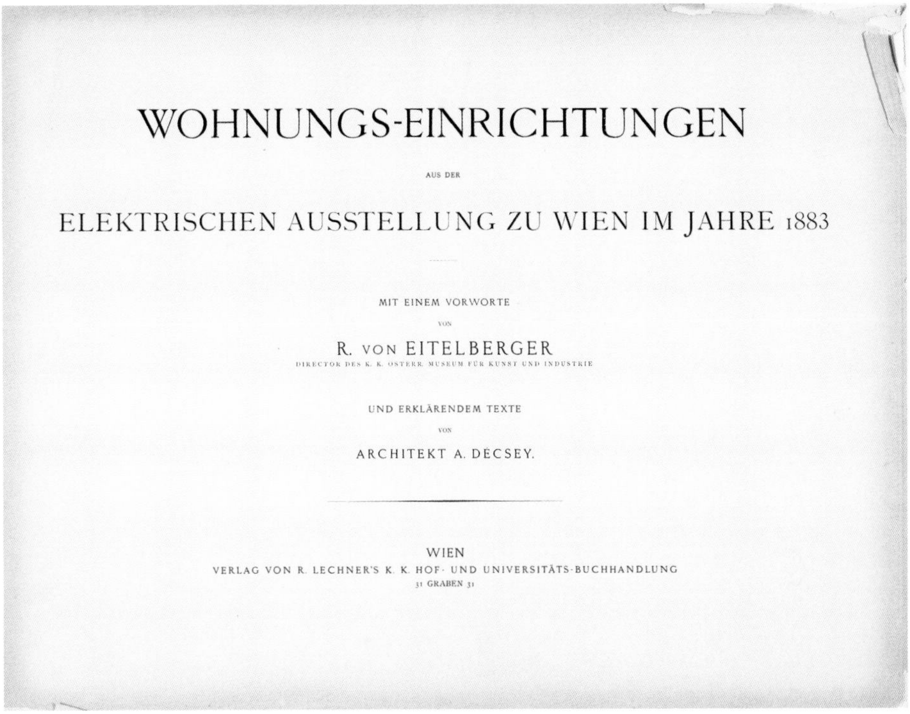

WOHNUNGS-EINRICHTUNGEN

AUS DER

ELEKTRISCHEN AUSSTELLUNG ZU WIEN IM JAHRE 1883

MIT EINEM VORWORTE

VON

R. VON EITELBERGER

DIRECTOR DES K. K. ÖSTERR. MUSEUM FÜR KUNST UND INDUSTRIE

UND ERKLÄRENDEM TEXTE

VON

ARCHITEKT A. DECSEY.

WIEN

VERLAG VON R. LECHNER'S K. K. HOF- UND UNIVERSITÄTS-BUCHHANDLUNG
31 GRABEN 31

7.4
*Wohnungs-einrichtungen aus der
Elektrischen Ausstellung zu Wien im
Jahre 1883*, title page.

Freud's Couch

ELEKTRISCHE AUSSTELLUNG WIEN 1883.

III.

Entworfen und ausgeführt von Alexander Albert.　　　　　　Fotografie von Ed. Türk, IV. Margarethenstr. 3, Wien.

HERRENZIMMER

VON ALEXANDER ALBERT, K. K. HOF-KUNSTTISCHLER IN WIEN.

Gesetzlich geschützt.　　　　　　Verlag von R. Lechner's k. k. Hof- und Universitäts-Buchhandlung in Wien.　　　　　　Déponé. Registered.

7.5
One of the model rooms visited by
Freud in 1883.

Figure 7.4 shows the title page of the published catalog of that exhibition, and figure 7.5 provides an example of one of the rooms he saw there. Several of these rooms were furnished with daybeds covered with kilims, as in the image in figure 7.8. (Note, on the left margin of the image in figure 7.5, a divan draped with kilims.) In letters to his fiancée Martha Bernays written in the summer of 1883, Freud states decisively that the furniture interested him more than the novel electric lighting.[10]

Freud's early-career interest in furnishings and interiors was no doubt piqued and informed by his treatment of several wealthy patients in their homes. Freud grew up in modest circumstances. His father was a wool merchant. His house calls in the 1880s to the palatial homes of fabulously rich patients like Anna von Lieben introduced him to the "haute bourgeois [sic] interiors of the Ringstrasse,"[11] though in all likelihood this path was at least partly prepared by his having attended the 1873 World Exposition in Vienna when he was seventeen.

Freud's divan, recently restored in London,[12] was a gift from his former patient Madame Benvenisti, given to him sometime around 1890.[13] He moved his home and professional office to Berggasse 19 in the same year as these couch portraits of the wildly popular actresses Sarah Bernhardt (figure 7.6) and Lily Langtry (figure 7.7), both posing as Cleopatra.

The kilim on Freud's couch, often referred to as "the Smyrna rug,"[14] was the gift in 1883 of Moritz Freud[15] on the occasion of Freud's engagement to Martha Bernays. Its presence there reflects the fact that kilims had by then become a favored decorative item in *fin-de-siècle* Western Europe (see figure 7.8).

In the early 1890s, Freud's interest in hypnosis began to wane; his practice shifted more toward the free association method and the pressure technique. By around 1900, he had given up on the pressure technique as well,[16] though he was then still recommending that patients keep their eyes closed while free-associating. However, this instruction, too, was soon eliminated.[17] Freud gradually shed one manipulation or directive after another as his stepwise transition from hypnosis to psychoanalysis unfolded.[18] But he did not explicitly describe the use of the couch as a standard element of his technique until the publication in 1904 of his brief paper "Freud's Psycho-Analytic Procedure."[19]

One might argue that Swales's analysis, focusing on the influence of some of Freud's first private patients, is compelling but incomplete. His narrow purview is finely wrought but limited in framing the couch's cultural context. Freud's earliest

7.6
Napoleon Sarony, Sarah Bernhardt
as Cleopatra, 1891.

7.7
Lily Langtry as Cleopatra, 1891.

"THE WOODBURYTYPE" LIGHT

MRS. LANGTRY AS CLEOPATRA

U. S. Copyright, 1891.

182 REGENT ST. W.

Freud's Couch

clinical experiences and the surrounding *Zeitgeist* of "orientalism" (to invoke Edward Said's famous coinage)[20] are only part of the picture. Freud's word for the couch, translated by Strachey as *sofa* in "On Beginning the Treatment,"[21] is *Ruhebett*, literally *resting bed* or *calm bed*, i.e., a daybed or (in French translations of Freud) *lit de repos*.[22] This term suggests a tie to asylum treatments, rest cures, sanatoria, and nineteenth-century psychiatric traditions of somatic and hypnotic treatment.

Recumbence unites Eros and Thanatos (see figure 7.9),[23] and fuses nineteenth-century therapeutics with modernism in design and architectural style.

7.8
George Hendrik Breitner, girl in a kimono, 1891.

7.9
Anonymous, dead child on a sofa, c. 1855.

7.10
The modernist style on display in a Thonet furniture catalog from the 1930s.

8

The Analyst's Moral Interior

Office décor inevitably reflects and communicates the analyst's social and moral values. Most contemporary analysts have distanced themselves from Freud's unabashed orientalist and archaeological motifs, preferring a more spartan, austere analytic couch that closely resembles the Greco-Roman dining couch. The analytic community thereby carries and contains a fractured representation of the ideal analytic couch.

D. W. Winnicott (1896–1971), the pediatrician turned psychoanalyst, famously declared that there is no such thing as a baby in the sense that "whenever one finds an infant one finds maternal care, and without maternal care there would be no infant."[1] Following his lead, we could say that the couch is a baby in the Winnicottian sense that there is no such thing as a couch without a *moral interior*.[2] The concept of the *moral interior* is invoked here to capture the sense in which aesthetic choices and sensibility express personal values. In other words, the design and décor of the analytic couch and the work space that envelopes and encases it are inseparable from the analyst *qua* analyst (see figures 8.1, 8.2, and 8.3). They form part of the analyst's nonverbally conveyed self-representation, and therefore function in the analytic situation on both an intrapsychic and interpersonal level.

The analyst's moral interior is, ineluctably, an enactment, a statement of desire and aesthetic values.[3] Décor reflects the analyst's witting or unwitting participation in an age-old debate about the moral meanings of appearance. The decoration of the domestic interior, like the adornment of the body, and like the history of reclining dining and the social history of recumbent posture, has always been indicative of moral and social values. Décor was held from at least the middle of the nineteenth century onward to reflect not only taste and social class, but also something deeper about the self—if not quite the health of the soul, then certainly its moral balance.[4] For critics such as John Ruskin (1819–1900), and in the U.S. the sisters Catharine Beecher (1800–1878) and Harriet Beecher Stowe (1811–1896), this included the condemnation of sham and the enshrinement of rustic simplicity.[5] This was part of romanticism's idealization of nature and naturalness. Ruskin held that ornament that falsifies the material of origin not only debases the quality of furniture and other domestic objects, but also is in and of itself immoral. Fake marble for columns, and painted *papier mâché* and *trompe-l'œil* wallpaper to represent plaster moldings, were repudiated, and the "honest" interior of the arts and crafts movement, epitomized by the country cottage, was valorized.[6]

8.1
Dan Welldon, the famous French
psychoanalyst André Green
(1927–2012) in his office, 2005.

8.2
Jerome Blackman's office and couch,
Virginia, 2016.

8.3
Shellburne Thurber, Brookline,
Massachusetts, analyst's office, 2000.

The Analyst's Moral Interior

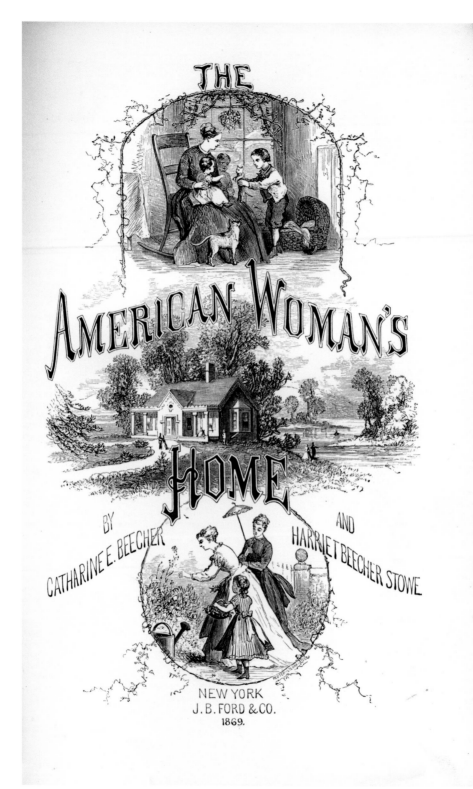

THE

AMERICAN WOMAN'S

HOME

BY CATHARINE E. BEECHER AND HARRIET BEECHER STOWE.

NEW YORK
J. B. FORD & CO.
1869.

8.4
Catharine Beecher and Harriet Beecher
Stowe, *The American Woman's Home*,
title page, 1869.

8.5
Freud's desk and couch in London, where
he moved in 1938, a year before his death,
to escape the Nazis.

This ethos was obviously at odds with Freud's aesthetic, though he perhaps shared its belief that newness is false or concealing.

When it comes to Freud, the term *moral interior* acquires a double meaning, for his professional space enacts and inculcates a theory of mind, conveying a "narrative of excavation," a "discourse of surface and strata,"[7] and an uncovering of hidden truths about the self. Freud and his contemporaries were riveted by the major archaeological finds of his epoch, and archaeology served Freud as a rich source of metaphors for psychoanalytic treatment.[8] In fact, Freud claimed to have read more archaeology than psychology.[9]

He began collecting antiquities shortly after his father's death in October 1896, and proceeded to surround himself with "disinterred objects" (death masks, funeral vases, bronze coffins, mummy portraits), creating a "space of loss and absence, grief and memory, elegy and mourning ... an exteriorized theater of [his] own emotional history"[10] (see figure 8.7). In other words, his collecting reflected his preoccupation with death; it was a kind of refined necrophilia.[11]

But Freud's collecting was also informed by his Enlightenment ideals: restoring value to discarded or neglected texts and objects, adding to a universal and public cultural heritage, and championing the value of remembering.[12] These ideals are instantiated and inculcated with the analyst's invitation to lie on the couch and free-associate.

So if it's true that Freud's patients, reclining on his bedlike Turkish divan, "cushioned by Eastern carpets, and wreathed in pungent [cigar] smoke ... find themselves at home in a late Victorian fantasy of the opium den,"[13] it's also true that they find themselves at an archaeological site where they are expected to disinter the past. Entering Freud's harem-necropolis, the analysand is enjoined to internalize Freud's understanding of the way the mind works. That's what the pressure technique (see figure 8.8 for a humorous depiction) sought to do, and that's why hypnosis was so important to Freud for such a long time.[14] Like collecting antiquities—or, for that matter, dreams, jokes, and slips of the tongue—psychoanalysis was, for Freud, crucially about memory and its preservation.[15]

Although today's typical analytic couch is much plainer, Freud's couch is very much in the style of the eighteenth-century *divan à la turque* or Turkish divan (see figures 8.9 and 8.10), a sofa or *chaise-longue* covered with oriental carpets and many cushions.[16]

8.6
Freud with some of his antiquities, c. 1905.

8.7
Freud's couch, surrounded by his antiquities, in Vienna, c. 1910–1920. Freud hung a large print of Abu Simbel above his couch.

"Perhaps this will refresh your memory, Mr. Conklin."

8.8
A 2001 cartoon from the *New Yorker* that could be viewed as a fond skewering of Freud's "pressure technique."

8.9
A divan-like couch covered with kilims in a German domestic interior, 1903.

8.10
Another couch with kilims, 1902; carpets adorn the walls as well, not unlike the way Freud had a carpet hung on the wall above his couch in Vienna (see figure 8.7).

The divan is (along with the ottoman) the iconic furnishing of the harem (see figure 8.11). However, Freud's procedure of seating himself behind and perpendicular to his recumbent interlocutor is a visual echo of the *canapé à confidents* (see figures 4.10, 4.11, and 4.12 above, and compare them to figures 8.12 and 8.13).

Freud's couch, with its pillows and rugs and blankets, is much more bedlike than the iconic analytic couch of more recent vintage. The form most strongly identified as the modern analytic couch (see figure 8.14) is a later, nineteenth-century design, an atavism of the Greco-Roman *klinē* (see figure 8.15).

8.11
Eugène Delacroix,
*The Women of Algiers
in Their Harem,*
1847–1849.

8.12
Freud seated behind his
couch, c. 1921.

8.13
Düsseldorf confidante, 1902.

8.14
Dresden *Ruhebank*, 1902.

8.15
Klinē monument of a boy, first century.

Culturally, enactment begets enactment. The iconic twentieth-century analytic couch is an aesthetic negation. It is plain, spartan, austere (see figures 8.16–8.21 for some examples from the consulting rooms of contemporary Latin American, North American, and European analysts)—a repudiation of Freud's luxuriant divan with its orientalist symbolic.

Austerity in office décor among some contemporary analysts reflects a distancing from Freud's exuberantly self-revelatory consultation-room motifs.[17] By today's standards, Freud's professional interior seems gregarious and loquacious. With his furnishings and antiquities representing, enacting, and inculcating an archaeological truth quest (if also a topographically driven attitude toward analytic work), Freud stands in contrast to today's more abstemious analysts, whose embrace of anonymity, practiced so imperfectly by the master, now sometimes shades into an enactment of self-erasure and a denial of subjectivity. Office asceticism concretizes anonymity. (Analysts could wear uniforms, like law enforcement officers or postal workers, but don't.)

8.16
Dan Welldon, Horacio Etchegoyen
(1919–2016), president of the International
Psychoanalytic Association from 1993 to
1997, behind his couch, Buenos Aires, 2007.

The Analyst's Moral Interior

The analytic community carries and contains a split representation of the couch: the iconic modern analytic couch unconsciously echoing the spare *klinē* or *lectum* of the Roman *convivium*, and Freud's plush Turkish divan surrounded by his antiquities, entombed in his libidinized necropolis. There is no incontrovertibly standard analytic couch—not because there are so many design choices, or because psychoanalysts are remarkably self-expressive, but because the couch is not a proprietary signifier like the stethoscope.[18] It is a cultural object with too long and complicated a genealogy for any single generation or community of analysts to be able to brand it.

8.17
Shellburne Thurber, Buenos Aires
analyst's couch, 2000.

8.18
Robert Tyson's couch, California, 2002.

8.19
Pearl King's (1918–2015) couch,
London, 2000.

8.20
Shellburne Thurber, Cambridge,
Massachusetts, analyst's couch, 2000.

8.21
Claudia Guderian, Ulrich Stuhr's couch,
Hamburg, Germany, 2002.

The Analyst's Moral Interior

9

Whence? Whither? Whether?

In the absence of formal empirical studies, no one can claim to know for whom or for what types of problem the use of the couch is best suited. Nevertheless, the couch—and recumbent speech itself—resonates with a culturally rich and intriguingly ambiguous interplay of traditions of luxury, healing, intimacy, and erotic freedom.

The earliest use of the couch in psychoanalysis was an enactment in which analyst and analysand took part in a ceremony that contextualized their joint enterprise, and assured them that they were traveling together along a path that was as well-worn as it was excitingly novel.

Today, the couch is not merely an icon for the nonpartaking public (see figure 9.1). It also serves the analytic dyad by reassuringly situating them in a clinical tradition that, while lacking empirical validation, nevertheless enjoys widespread cultural validation vouchsafed by the couch's iconic status.

The analyst's invitation to lie on the couch can be seen as a form of ritual initiation, not merely in the sense of a routinized procedure, but also in the deeper sense of "a deliberate dislocation or disorientation of self" that is part of an "epiphanic rite of passage toward deeper self-knowledge."[1] The analytic couch has become the emblem of a cultural narrative of self-discovery.[2]

9.1
New York City subway poster, 1991.

9.2
Anonymous, study of female
nude, 1853.

9.3
August is "a bad month,"
New Yorker cover, 2004.

9.4
"August on the Cape,"
New Yorker cartoon, 2009.

Whence? Whither? Whether?

The analyst's *moral interior* (see chapter 8) incites *and* tames the sexuality of intimate discourse. It mediates transgression (see figure 9.2) and separation (see figures 9.3 and 9.4).

Within classical psychoanalytic theories of therapy, the transgressive potential of recumbence (see figures 9.5 and 9.6) was offset by the codification of the technical precepts of neutrality, abstinence, and anonymity, such that the couch became a locus of both intimacy *and* distancing.[3] In the relationship between analyst and analysand, closeness and distance are, in part, regulated by posture. Clinically, this translates into a dynamic, fluctuating balance that analysts take for granted at their peril.

9.5
E. J. Bellocq, New Orleans prostitute, c. 1912. Note how the subject is posed on precisely the type of *chaise-longue* or daybed that is today identified as the typical analytic couch, as seen in figures 8.14 and 8.16–8.21 above.

9.6
Confessions of a Psychiatrist, cover illustration, 1954.

EVERY BOUDOIR WAS HIS OFFICE:
EVERY PATIENT HIS PLAYTHING —

CONFESSIONS of a
PSYCHIATRIST

35¢
B 184

by Henry Lewis Nixon

A BEACON FIRST AWARD ORIGINAL NOVEL!

9.7
René Magritte, *Mme Récamier de David*,
1951 (cf. figure 4.1).

All analysts reckon with the twin hazards of seductiveness and deadness (see figure 9.7).

Analysts who have lost touch with its transgressive potential will find the couch antiquated or superfluous. But recumbent speech, with its obvious yet all too easily repressed strangeness, will always retain its transgressive valence.[4] The analytic couple is a transgressive couple. Together, analyst and analysand are boundary violators;[5] in fantasy and in what they are able to say to one another, they break social norms of conversation in the service of becoming a creative couple. It would be foolish to think that recumbence and sexuality could ever be separated when in fact not even in death do they part (see figures 9.8 and 9.9).[6]

The history of the couch reminds us of its rootedness in traditions of suffering, healing (see figure 9.10), intimacy, and their vital expressions in art (see figure 9.11) as well as in design and decoration.

9.8
Etruscan sarcophagus,
525–500 BCE.

9.9
Tomb of Eleanor of
Aquitaine and
Henry II, c. 1210.

9.10
Asclepius healing a youth, fifth century BCE.
The patient reclines on the traditional *klinē*
(see chapter 2).

9.11
Pablo Picasso, *Nu couché*, 1942.

Whence? Whither? Whether?

It should be clear that describing the use of the couch as an enactment in no way vitiates its clinical utility when properly prescribed. But just as free- associating is a technology, the use of the couch is a technique; neither is an analytic goal in itself.[7] Analysts who routinely or automatically prescribe the use of the couch risk a conformism that could eventuate in a simulacrum of analysis.[8]

The empirical status of frequency and posture remains unexplored. Are there specific problems for which use of the couch is especially helpful? Are there specific indications and contraindications for its use? What about where analyst positions him- or herself relative to the patient on the couch? Does the "choreography" of the analytic setup matter?[9]

These are research questions awaiting formal study. Meanwhile, the profession relies on clinical tradition and the empiricism of the individual practitioner, who is justified in viewing whatever facilitates an analytic process as sound technique.[10] It seems unlikely that anyone would maintain that a person would need to be lying on a couch to engage in self-analytic work of any kind. At the same time, it is hard to imagine anyone doing clinical analytic work without the luxury of contact with his or her own inner reverie and the opportunity to contain countertransference that the patient's use of the couch affords the analyst.[11] Therefore, it would be odd, at this point in time, to mandate or discourage its use.[12]

9.12
New York City subway
poster, 1991.

Can one indeed find the "*same* peace of mind sitting in a pew," as the advertisement in figure 9.12 suggests? Unlikely. Different peace of mind, maybe, as the text at the top of the image in figure 9.13 indicates.

The use of the couch can open the door to an oddly powerful discourse of the self that can't be had elsewhere. The function and meaning of recumbent speech are key to this discourse. Recumbent speech transcends free association in that it authorizes a mode of intrapsychic and interpersonal luxuriation. Recumbent speech allows for an experience of selfhood that simply has no parallel anywhere in the social world.

Nevertheless, this fact has not stopped some analysts from launching attacks on the use of the couch. As noted in chapter 1, the couch has been derided—*from within the profession*—as infantilizing to the analysand, avoidant on the analyst's part of conflict or hostility, and obstructing analyst and analysand from authentic engagement with one another.[13] These are problematic assertions because they all assume a frozen, rigid, doctrinaire, or overly detached stance on the part of the analyst rather than an effort to sense what's going on and adapt technique accordingly. But even more insidiously, these denigrations of recumbent speech constitute attacks on privacy and freedom—both the analysand's and the analyst's.

following pages

9.13
Psychoanalysis (comic book magazine)
inaugural issue cover illustration
describing "People Searching for Peace of
Mind through Psychoanalysis," 1955.

9.14
Psychoanalysis, 1955. Page 1 introduces
the psychiatrist-psychoanalyst who
will be the hero of the story throughout the
three case histories presented in issue 1.
Note that the hero's office décor is
described in the text's opening lines as
"tasteful" and "subdued." His *klinē*-like
couch is of the variety most strongly
associated with twentieth- and twenty-
first-century psychoanalytic practice
(cf. figures 8.14, 8.16–8.21, and 9.5).

THIS IS A **PSYCHIATRIST!** INTO HIS PEACEFUL, TASTEFULLY- DECORATED, SUBDUED OFFICE COME **THE** TORMENTED AND THE DRIVEN, SEEKING TO UNRAVEL THE TANGLED EMOTIONAL SKEINS THAT CLOUD AND KNOT THEIR BROKEN LIVES. SKILLFULLY GUIDED BY HIM PAST THE SUB-SURFACE REEFS OF FEARS AND GUILTS AND ANXIETIES, HIS PATIENTS EVENTUALLY DISCOVER FOR THEMSELVES THE COURSE TO SELF-UNDERSTANDING, PEACE AND TRUE PERSONAL HAPPINESS WHICH LIES LIKE A RICH TREASURE WAITING TO BE UNEARTHED. AND THE *MAP* TO THIS TREASURE...THE *KEY* TO ITS LOCK...IS *FOUND* THROUGH...

PSYCHOANALYSIS

THE PSYCHIATRIST IS WAITING NOW FOR THE *FIRST* OF *THREE NEW PATIENTS* WHO WILL COME TO HIM IN THIS ISSUE FOR *HELP.* WE WILL MEET THEM AND FOLLOW THEIR TREATMENT *TOGETHER. READY?* THEN LET'S OPEN THE FILE ON...

What might prompt psychoanalysts to denigrate one of the core features of their own craft? Writing in 1846, the Danish philosopher Søren Kierkegaard (1813–1855) presciently stated that "ours is the age of advertisement and publicity."[14] In such an age of self-exposure and hypertransparency (see figure 9.15), privacy and private expression are devalued, and a form of perverse egalitarianism becomes the new piety. Kierkegaard called this a *leveling* process through which people seek to avert envy. He averred that "if distinction could be shown to be purely fictitious then everyone would be prepared to admire it."[15] No one is admired unless he or she can also be ridiculed.

This leveling process is actually a cultural therapy of envy operating on the plane of the collective unconscious. In the present age, our digital age, googling one's therapist is not transgressive, googling is the norm; it is privacy that is transgressive. To amplify Kierkegaard's insight: in an antiauthoritarian, egalitarian age of hypertransparency, it is harder to preserve the transgressive space for privacy and interiority. Because of an internalized leveling process, epitomized by attacks on the use of the couch by psychoanalysts themselves, the analytic couple is at risk for assaulting its own privacy, which is felt to be transgressive in accordance with social norms. A dismissive attitude toward the use of the couch can be rationalized by facile appeals to the dynamics of power and submission.[16]

The use of the couch can be said to aid or inhibit free association, to facilitate or discourage the exploration of shame dynamics, to promote or obstruct the development of authentic interpersonal engagement between analyst and analysand. In other words, it can be said to be regressive and infantilizing or empowering and liberating. But the same could be said about almost any aspect of psychoanalytic technique. Any psychotherapeutic intervention can be experienced as authoritarian if conveyed prematurely, insensitively, or clumsily. A priori assumptions about how analysands will experience the use of the couch are unwarranted. In psychoanalytic treatment, analyst and analysand are tasked with maintaining a spirit of open inquiry in which all aspects of the experience of analysis, including its methods and procedures, can be discussed.

For the working clinical psychoanalyst, the couch is a locus of rich contradiction and generative tension—between abstinence and transgression, ceremony and spontaneity, renunciation and comfort, self-scrutiny and fantasy. On the couch, the analysand engages in the hard work and luxurious freedom of recumbent speech.

Despite some contemporary analysts' ambivalence, the couch endures as a symbol of interiority and self-reflection. The genealogy and iconography of the couch help explain its continued cultural resonance even at a time when psychoanalysis has waned in popularity as a treatment modality. From the Greco-Roman ideals of pleasure and leisure to the reclamation of recumbent speech following the French Revolution, and from the couch's emergence in the nineteenth century as a fixture of TB sanatoria to its transformation into a key element of modernist design and metonym for comfort and relaxation, the couch persists as a complex signifier of subjectivity and individuality.

"*I love talking to you about my problems. We should do a podcast.*"

9.15
Self-exposure and hypertransparency in the present age.

Notes

Preface

1. The term *psy disciplines* is borrowed from Rose (1996).

Chapter 1

1. See Lable et al. (2010); Schacter and Kächele (2010); Roose (2012).

2. Freud (1913).

3. The British psychoanalyst W. R. Bion (1897–1979) developed the concept of the analyst's capacity for reverie and containment (Bion 1967; 1970). Containment refers to the analyst's ability (sometimes disrupted) to take in and transform a patient's most intense and painful affects, guided in part by the analyst's reverie, which allows for the metabolism, creative elaboration, and helpful articulation in interpretation of the difficult aspects of a patient's emotional experience. Bion (1967) thought of the analyst's capacity for reverie as analogous to maternal reverie, the mother's way of understanding the preverbal baby's needs and wants. The analyst, seated behind the recumbent patient and freed from attending to the ordinary social cues of a face-to-face interaction, is better able to access a more imaginative and generative mode of listening. For a brief synopsis of these ideas, and some superb examples of how a contemporary analyst employs them in her clinical work, see LaFarge (2000). Brown (2011) provides a fuller explication of current Bionian thought and its application to clinical theory and technique. Bion's concept of reverie can also be viewed as an amplification of Freud's (1912) precept concerning the analyst's evenly suspended or free-floating attention.

4. Fairbairn (1958); Stern (1978). W. R. D. Fairbairn's (1889–1964) major contributions are collected in his *Psychoanalytic Studies of the Personality* (1952). Guntrip (1975) describes periods of lying and sitting during his analysis with Fairbairn. Melanie Klein (1882–1960), the doyenne of object relations theory, adhered to Freud's recommended technique in her treatment of adults.

5. Kelman (1954) claims that "There is phylogenetic and ontogenetic evidence to support the view that the reclining, supine position is closer to what came first, is more primitive, or closer to our essentialness. The extensor groups of muscles are earlier and more highly developed phylogenetically" (66).

6. Several authors have sought to interpret this stipulation in terms of Freud's personality or biography. Gilman (1993) has cited in this connection Freud's attitude toward being Jewish; Lichtenberg (1995) posits Freud's aversion to shame dynamics—a point echoed by Forrest (2004). Friedberg and Linn (2012) attribute it to Freud's "unresolved scoptophilic conflicts" (38). Schacter and Kächele (2010) allege that Freud preferred the couch so as to minimize patients' expressions of anger (443) and to "protect" himself from dissent

(442, 453). Roazen (1975) similarly implies a hypersensitivity to criticism on Freud's part, leading to a wish to avoid face-to-face interaction. Echoing Robertiello (1967), Jacobson (1995) calls the use of the couch "an accident of history" (304), while Greenberg (2001) describes it as "the first recorded example of an unexamined countertransference enactment rationalized in terms of its technical advantages" (422). See also Stern (1978), who cites literature on recumbence and spontaneity, and on perceptual isolation and vividness of dreams. Perhaps these comments are insightful, but none seeks to situate the use of the couch in its wider cultural context, as I shall seek to do in what follows. Arguments for and against the use of the couch in psychoanalysis today are reviewed by Lable et al. (2010).

7. See Stern (1978).

8. Celenza (2005) notes its fetishization; Forrest (2004) has been among its disparagers. Friedberg and Linn (2012) are among recent authors who are skeptical about the value of the use of the couch. Schacter and Kächele (2010) are among those who believe that the couch entrains passivity and submission, leaving the analyst to "enjoy the relative superiority, authority, and power of his or her position" (448). They assume that face-to-face analysis "optimizes" authenticity (451). Roazen (1975), too, assumes that the couch entails submission. Cf. Ross (1999) on the antiauthoritarian aspects of the traditional psychoanalytic setup.

9. See, for example, Aruffo (1995); Goldberger (1995); Sadow (1995).

10. Robertiello (1967) heaps scorn upon the use of the couch as "a truly ridiculous anachronism" (71). More recently, Forrest (2004) espouses a similar view, with which I strongly disagree. In my view, people undergoing analysis usually have many reactions to recumbence and varying experiences of using the couch. The meaning of recumbent posture is not fixed or categorical; it shifts as analysand and analyst try to allow it to unfold. Some patients might experience lying on the couch as a submission, but it is often helpful to examine that response and see if it changes and evolves into other responses. It doesn't make sense to claim to know in advance that lying on the couch will be experienced as infantilizing, or that any given response to the couch will be permanent. (I return to these issues in chapter 9.) For an interesting take on the shifting experiences of security and anxiety related to the use of the couch, see Balint (1959), esp. 92–94.

11. Greencacre (1954), for example, notes that already by her time "to many lay people" the couch had become "the main or only index of whether the treatment was psychoanalytic" (635). Her contemporary Kelman (1954) writes: "The Analytic Couch not only has come to symbolize analysis, it has been considered to be analysis" (65).

12. Freud (1913), 133–134 (emphases added).

13. The translation is James Strachey's in *The Standard Edition of the Complete Psychological Works of Sigmund Freud* (London: Hogarth Press, 1953–1974). See chapter 7, note 22 below.

Chapter 2

1. Gloag (1966), 78.

2. The quote is from Brunner (2013), 79. He goes on to explain that "In general, early humans likely prepared places to sleep from stone, wood, or earth and covered them with layers of fur, leaves, grass, moss, or straw to make them more comfortable" (80), though early humans didn't necessarily sleep lying down.

3. Brunner (2013), 81.

4. Liddell and Scott ([1871] 1935).

5. See especially Books II and X of the *Republic*. Berger (2016) provides an analysis of the "Klinopolis" or "Couch City" discussed by Socrates in this context.

6. This description again follows Brunner (2013), 82.

7. The discussion in this paragraph draws upon the work of Roller (2006) and Dunbabin (2003).

8. The Greek word συμπόσιον (*symposion*), whose more familiar Latin cognate is *symposium*, is derived from the word for fellow-drinker (συμπότης) and the verb to drink together (συμπίνειν). The classic example is Plato's *Symposium* (c. 385–370 BCE).

9. The quotations here are from Dunbabin (2003), 13 and 202.

10. Roller (2006).

11. Ibid., 176. As Roller explains, there were three paths toward manumission in ancient Rome: (1) decreed by master; (2) freed in the master's last will and testament; (3) freedom purchased by slaves themselves.

12. Rudofsky (1980), 26.

13. Gowers (2006), 7.

14. Rudofsky (1980).

15. The drinking of four cups of wine during the Passover *seder* probably represents a vestige of the Greek *symposion*.

16. This point is made by Roller (2006). I use the words recumbent, reclining, and supine interchangeably. Supine and prone are antonyms, the latter denoting "lying face downwards or on the belly" (*OED*).

17. Kelman (1954); Rieff (1979). Ross (1999) cites George Klein's dictum: "posture is perception" (92).

18. Roller (2006).

19. Rybczynski (1986).

20. Gloag (1966); Pardailhé-Galabrun (1991). Throughout Europe in the medieval period and early Renaissance, "The bed was a prestige item, as literature, painting, and notarial

records show" (Duby 1988, 184). It was also "almost the only item of furniture ever be-queathed to a loyal servant, a needy relative, or a hospital" (ibid., 490).

21. Adapted from the *Oxford English Dictionary*. The French word *douane* for custom house also descends from the Arabic *divan*, a further illustration of the word's legal, official, and political connotations.

22. For scholarship on the *lit de justice*, see Hanley (1983), Holt (1988), and Fraser (2006). See also Duby (1988), 491. On the last *lit de justice*, see Schama (1989).

Chapter 3

1. Wright (1962), 40.

2. From the *Oxford English Dictionary* (*OED*). The quote from 1576 is by an author named Fleming. Further examples in the *OED* from Bacon (1605), Milton (1667), and others illustrate the same ambiguity in usage throughout the sixteenth and seventeenth centuries. See also Duby (1988).

3. See Campbell (1999), 327.

4. Rybczynski (1986), 83.

5. Ibid., 84. See also Thornton (1984).

6. Rybczynski (1986), 95. Hooped skirts became fashionable in the second decade of eighteenth-century France, forcing *menuisiers* to set back the arms of their chairs to accommodate the fullness of these skirts (Verlet, 1991).

7. See Talbott (2002); DeJean (2009).

8. The quotations are from DeJean (2009), 115, 124.

9. Pardailhé-Galabrun (1991), 101. The word *sofa* exists in French, German, Italian, Spanish, Portuguese, and English.

10. Verlet (1991).

11. The term *contingent causation* is borrowed from Gaddis (2002).

Chapter 4

1. We shall return to the problematic intersection of healing, eroticism, and transgressive potential in chapter 9. The figure of the lecherous male doctor with his bedridden or otherwise supine female patient obviously long antedates the advent of psychoanalysis. Nevertheless, it is unfortunately echoed in the figure of the seated male analyst with his recumbent female analysand insofar as the early history of psychoanalysis is riddled with boundary violations so configured.

2. See Kasson (1990); Talbott (2002); DeJean (2009).

3. Rybczynski (1986); Pardailhé-Galabrun (1991); DeJean (2009).

4. Rybczynski (1986); Pardailhé-Galabrun (1991).

5. Less than 10 percent of mid-eighteenth-century Parisian mansions (*hôtels*) had specialized "bath" rooms, but by 1801 approximately 30 percent of luxurious dwellings built since 1770 had them (Pardailhé-Galabrun, 1991).

6. Pardailhé-Galabrun (1991).

7. Ibid. Sir John Harrington's water closet dates to 1596, but the Bramah Valve Closet, a toilet bowl with a water seal to block cesspool odors, was invented in 1778 (Rybczynski 1986). The most important changes in this regard did not occur until the second half of the nineteenth century and the early twentieth century. Parisians did not have indoor drinking water until 1860; the installation of gas and electricity began in Paris in 1878; water mains in 1883 (Pardailhé-Galabrun 1991); flush toilets were uncommon until the mid-1880s (Perrot 1990). The mass production of flush toilets was begun by London plumber Thomas Crapper in the 1860s (DeJean 2009). A French census documents that in 1886 more than 40 percent of homes in Marseille had no system for waste disposal (Perrot 1990). In general, before 1890 central heating, indoor plumbing, running hot and cold water, electric light and power, and elevators were uncommon or unavailable; by 1920 all of these were widely available (Rybczynski 1986).

8. DeJean (2009).

9. On this perspective in clothing history, see, for example, Davenport (1948) and Boucher (1987).

10. The discussion here follows DeJean (2009), 139.

11. Trevor-Roper (1969); Midelfort (1972); Roper (2004).

12. See in this connection Belinda Jack's (2012) excellent exposition of the history of the woman reader.

Chapter 5

1. Campbell (1999).

2. Figures 5.13 and 5.14 present us with a *triclinium* revenant! (See chapter 2.) *Plus ça change, plus c'est la même chose.*

3. Ibid.

4. Streptomycin, rifampin, and iproniazid were introduced in the 1950s. Through serendipity, it was TB that brought psychiatry the monoamine oxidase inhibitors, the class of antidepressant medications known as the MAOIs, following the chance observation of improvement in symptomatic depression in tubercular patients treated with iproniazid.

5. Campbell (1999).

6. Ibid.; Talbott (2002).

7. Campbell (1999).

8. Talbott (2002), 126.

9. Housholder (1974); Speert (1973); Talbott (2002).

10. Mayer (2006), 49.

11. Talbott (2002). In other words, peak production occurred precisely at the time Freud began using the couch in his pre-psychoanalytic (hypnotic) treatments (see chapter 6).

12. These included Josef Hoffmann, Jean Prouvé, Charlotte Perriand, Le Corbusier, Mies van der Rohe, Marcel Breuer, Alvar Aalto, and Serge Chermayeff (Campbell 1999; Campbell 2005).

Chapter 6

1. *Alienist* was an early term for psychiatrist or specialist in the treatment of people deemed "insane." For a more complete discussion of the term, see Makari (2015), 382–383.

2. On the origins of the term, and the emergence of nineteenth-century hypnosis and hypnotic therapeutics from mesmerism, see Kravis (1988).

3. For an authoritative statement on this matter by a leading late-nineteenth-century and early-twentieth-century practitioner of hypnosis, see Forel (1906).

4. Freud (1886; 1888–1889; 1892–1894). Jean-Martin Charcot (1825–1893) took up the study of hypnotism in 1878. Charcot and his followers at the Salpêtrière saw suggestibility as a hallmark of hysteria made evident by susceptibility to hypnosis. Ambroise Auguste Liébeault (1823–1904) and his followers in the rival Nancy school viewed suggestibility as a universal human trait. Liébeault's views were popularized by Hippolyte Bernheim (1840–1919) in the 1880s. Bernheim (1888; [1891] 1980) declared that hypnosis merely augments normal suggestibility. See Kravis (1988). For a superb history of the wider development of psychoanalysis out of its nineteenth-century European context, see Makari (2008).

5. On this point, see Mayer (2006; 2013). See also Freud's impassioned review of Forel's book on the subject (Freud 1889).

6. Mayer (2006), 49.

7. Swaan (1977). Swaan comments that these trends in office-based private practice in Vienna "were similar and roughly synchronous to those in German cities" (385).

8. Freud (1925), 16.

9. Freud (1888), 55.

10. Monell (1900); Kellogg (1910).

Chapter 7

1. Breuer and Freud (1895).

2. Freud (1901).

3. See, for example, his comments to this effect in Breuer and Freud (1895, esp. 108–109) and Freud (1910).

4. Swales (1986), 52.

5. Swales (1986) posits morphine withdrawal as a possible iatrogenic factor in the etiology of her hysterical symptoms.

6. Ibid.

7. Swales (1986), 74–75n62.

8. Ibid.

9. The evidence here is somewhat ambiguous. In an 1891 article for a medical dictionary, Freud describes placing the patient "in a comfortable chair" (Freud 1891, 108). On the other hand, the patient described in "A Case of Successful Treatment by Hypnotism" (Freud 1892–1893) is unquestionably recumbent during his treatment of her.

10. I am indebted to Eric Anderson, PhD, of the Rhode Island School of Design (RISD) for drawing this to my attention.

11. Sarnitz and Scholz-Strasser (2015), 11.

12. See Collins (2013).

13. Fuss (2004); Swales (1986); Warner (2011).

14. Scholars disagree about whether this rug was indeed a gift or a purchase. Warner (2011) says it was an engagement gift, and writes that "Experts have since identified the rug as a Ghashgha'i piece (not from Smyrna, as Freud thought), woven farther east by that great nomadic tribe who herd sheep and goats in the changing prairies and valleys of Fars province, on the borders of Iran and Turkey" (415). Burke (2006), however, asserts that it is an Iranian Qashqai (or Ghashgha'i) rug that Freud purchased in 1891 at an exhibition at the Austrian Trade Museum.

15. Moritz Freud was a cousin of Sigmund Freud and a merchant in Salonika; he married Freud's sister Marie ("Mitzi") in March 1887.

16. See Breuer and Freud (1895), 110–111fn1.

17. Freud (1904).

18. Swaan (1977).

19. Freud (1904). This point is made by Mayer (2006).

20. Said (1978).

21. Freud (1913).

22. Freud's usage in the *Gesammelte Werke* includes *Divan, Diwan, Kanapee, Ruhebett*, and *Sofa*, but not *Couch*. Strachey's translation for all these terms in the *Standard Edition of the Complete Psychological Works of Sigmund Freud* is *sofa*. The word *couch* does not appear in the *Standard Edition* as a noun, only as a verb. The term for *couch* used in contemporary French translations of Freud, including the PUF translation supervised by Laplanche, is *lit de repos*. Contemporary German parlance includes the words *die Couch* (fem.), *der Diwan* (masc.), *das Kanapee, das Sofa* (both neut.) A typical expression today is "Ich bin reif für die Couch," literally: I'm ripe for the couch, meaning I'm so exhausted or down that I need a break. It does not mean that I need professional help. But "Sie ist ein

Notes

Fall für die Couch"—literally: She is a case for the couch—means: She (really) needs psychotherapy.

23. It is estimated that 3 million daguerreotypes were made per year in the U.S. through the 1840s, and even more in the 1850s (Grier 1988). This is an impressive figure given that according to the 1850 census, the U.S. population was 23 million, including 3 million slaves. Daguerreotypes cost 25 cents in the 1850s. For most nineteenth-century American families, the post-mortem daguerreotype was the first and only portrait of a deceased child (Burns 1990). The rate of survival of children to age 10 was 74 percent from 1640 to 1760, but *dropped* to 50 percent or less during the nineteenth century (Burns 1990).

Chapter 8

1. Winnicott ([1960] 1965), 39n1.

2. The term *moral interior* is drawn from Snodin and Howard (1996), 147.

3. By the analyst's *moral interior* I mean the analyst's *enacted* (nonverbally communicated) moral sensibility. How and where enacted? Aesthetically, in the analyst's consulting room. It should be clear that by *moral* I'm not referring to ethical conduct, to good or bad behavior; nor am I referring to countertransference enactments and their role in the analytic process. Rather, I'm referring to a nonverbal form of self-disclosure: the moral and social values conveyed in appearance and enacted in office décor and furnishings as well as in the analyst's apparel and deportment.

4. See Snodin and Howard (1996).

5. Beecher and Stowe (1869).

6. Snodin and Howard (1996).

7. These quotes are from O'Donoghue (2004), 655 and 662.

8. See Gamwell and Wells (1989), Kuspit (1989), Forrester (1994), and O'Donoghue (2004). Freud was 17 years old when Schliemann made his first major finds at Troy in 1873. Tutankhamun's tomb was discovered in 1922, when Freud was 66.

9. Freud said so in a 1931 letter to Stefan Zweig (quoted by Forrester 1994).

10. Fuss (2004), 79. Freud eventually acquired nearly 2,000 objects, mostly sculpture, most of them Egyptian, but also Greek, Roman, Near Eastern, and Asian (Gamwell and Wells 1989).

11. Cf. Kuspit (1989).

12. See Forrester (1994).

13. Fuss (2004), 90.

14. See Kravis (1988).

15. Forrester (1994).

16. Verlet (1991).

17. Analysts' ambivalence toward the analytic situation is a topic I have explored in greater detail elsewhere (Kravis 2013a; 2013b).

18. In the heyday of American psychoanalysis in the 1950s and 1960s, and to some extent even into the 1970s and 1980s, many academic psychiatrists and psychologists who were not psychoanalysts nevertheless furnished their offices with couches. In this respect the couch was a pan-professional signifier reaching across the *psy* disciplines.

Chapter 9

1. Sherwin (2011), 116–117. "The initiation of the rite of passage also goes under the ancient Greek rubric of *ekphrasis*—bringing the initiate across an epistemological and existential threshold, from one reality to another, through an experience, an event, an epiphany, that affords transformative insight" (Sherwin 2011, 217n120).

2. The term *cultural narrative* is borrowed from Kirschner (1996).

3. See Goldberger (1995). Klauber (1981) emphasizes the distancing aspects of the patient's recumbence, which, he says, offsets the intimacy of the analytic discourse (see especially 51). Kelman's (1954) truncated discussion under the subheading "Analyst's neurotic needs for the couch position" (75) is unpersuasive, but deserves recognition as an early attempt to express the notion that both analyst and analysand can use the couch to regulate closeness and distance.

4. The sentiment that psychoanalysis is transgressive is conveyed in the commonly expressed notion that analytic treatment is incredibly self-indulgent, extravagant, and wasteful.

5. Needless to say, actual boundary violations by analysts are unprofessional, harmful, and antianalytic.

6. Ariès (1962) discusses Elizabethan mortuary sculpture featuring side-by-side recumbent figures as an early form of family portraiture.

7. The same point is made by Aruffo (1995).

8. This presents a special problem for analytic training insofar as candidates are made to feel that their supervised analyses must conform as closely as possible to a standardized or orthodox image of what an analysis "should" look like to outside observers (supervisors, Progression or Education Committees, etc.). This pressures candidate-analysts into automatic or premature prescription of the use of the couch, and might lead to feelings of failure if an analysand sits up (Kulish 1996; Lable et al. 2010). Optimally, candidates should feel freer to explore analytically with any given analysand the meanings and advantages and disadvantages for both parties involved in the use of the couch. (A similar view is expressed by Celenza 2005. For an early example of advocacy for a flexible approach toward the use of the couch—written, surprisingly, in an era of psychoanalytic orthodoxy—see Kelman 1954.)

9. This issue is discussed in detail by Kelman (1954) and thoughtfully reconsidered by Carlson (2002). Kulish (1996) reviews the literature on resistance to the use of the couch,

and traditional notions in older psychoanalytic publications about incapacity and contra-indications to its use. She then offers her own sensitively reported and clinically useful case example.

10. Ogden (1996).

11. The observation that the patient's use of the couch affords the analyst greater opportunity to contain countertransference is mentioned by Gedo (1995).

12. Skolnick (2015) rightly critiques "the definitive pairing of psychoanalysis with the required use of the couch" (630). At the same time, however, he constructs a straw man argument against those who supposedly view the use of the couch as the sine qua non of establishing an analytic process (634 and *passim*).

13. See, for example, Forrest (2004), Schacter and Kächele (2010), Friedberg and Linn (2012), and Skolnick (2015). A much earlier (and often cited) author writing in this vein is Robertiello (1967).

14. Kierkegaard ([1846] 1962), 6.

15. Ibid., 18–19. Kierkegaard added that people are all too ready "to admire in public what is considered unimportant in private" (9).

16. Communally, this is illustrated by the recent attacks on the use of couch *from within* psychoanalysis. I'm not talking about the commonsense precepts of flexibility, of exploring nonjudgmentally and analytically a patient's reluctance to use the couch when recommended, or Goldberger's (1995) elegant observations about how the couch can be used defensively. I'm talking about analysts who, wrapping themselves in the egalitarian mantle of today's *Zeitgeist*, purport to know that the couch is a relic of an authoritarian era, and hold its use to be, a priori, infantilizing to patients or avoidant of authentic connection.

References

SE = *The Standard Edition of the Complete Psychological Works of Sigmund Freud*, 24 vols., ed. and trans. J. Strachey, in collaboration with A. Freud. London: Hogarth Press and the Institute of Psycho-Analysis, 1953–1974.

Ariès, P. 1962. *Centuries of Childhood: A Social History of Family Life*. R Baldick, trans. New York: Knopf.

Aruffo, R. N. 1995. The Couch: Reflections from an Interactional View of Analysis. *Psychoanal Inq* 15: 369–385.

Balint, M. 1959. *Thrills and Regressions.* Madison, CT: International Universities Press.

Barwise, S. 1916. A Note on the Derbyshire Sanatorium. *Brit J Tuberculosis* 10(3): 126–131.

Beecher, C. E., and Stowe, H. B. 1869. *The American Woman's Home.* New York: J. B. Ford.

Berger, H. 2016. Couch City: The Discourse of the Couch in Plato's "Republic." https://www.academia.edu/2518590/Couch_City_The_Discourse_of_the_Couch_in_Platos_Republic (accessed August 24, 2016).

Bernheim, H. 1888. *Suggestive Therapeutics: A Treatise on the Nature and Uses of Hypnotism.* C. A. Herter, trans. New York: G. P. Putnam's Sons.

Bernheim, H. [1891] 1980. *Hypnotism, Suggestion, and Psychotherapy: New Studies*. R. S. Sander, trans. New York: International Universities Press.

Bion, W. R. 1967. *Second Thoughts: Selected Papers on Psycho-Analysis.* London: William Heinemann Medical Books.

Bion, W. R. 1970. *Attention and Interpretation.* London: Tavistock.

Boucher, F. 1987. *20,000 Years of Fashion: The History of Costume and Personal Adornment.* New York: Abrams.

Breuer, J., and Freud, S. 1895. *Studies on Hysteria.* **SE 2**

Brown, L. J. 2011. *Intersubjective Processes and the Unconscious: An Integration of Freudian, Kleinian and Bionian Perspectives.* London: Routledge.

Brunner, B. 2013. *The Art of Lying Down: A Guide to Horizontal Living.* L. Lantz, trans. Brooklyn: Melville House.

Burke, J. 2006. *The Gods of Freud: Sigmund Freud's Art Collection.* Knopf Australia.

Burns, S. B. 1990. *Sleeping Beauty: Memorial Photography in America.* Altadena, CA: Twelvetrees Press.

Campbell, M. 1999. From Cure Chair to *Chaise Longue*: Medical Treatment and the Form of the Modern Recliner. *J Des Hist* 12(4): 327–343.

Campbell, M. 2005. What Tuberculosis Did for Modernism: The Influence of a Curative Environment on Modernist Design and Architecture. *Med Hist* 49(4): 463–488.

Carlson, D. A. 2002. Free-Swinging Attention. *Psychoanal Q* 71: 725–750.

Celenza, A. 2005. Vis-à-vis the Couch: Where is Psychoanalysis? *Int J Psychoanal* 86: 1645–1659.

Charlish, A., ed. 1976. *The History of Furniture.* London: Orbis.

Collins, L. 2013. London Postcard: Fixer-upper. *New Yorker*, December 2, 23–24.

Davenport, M. 1948. *The Book of Costume.* New York: Crown Publishers.

DeJean, J. 2009. *The Age of Comfort: When Paris Discovered Casual—and the Modern Home Began.* New York: Bloomsbury.

Duby, G., ed. 1988. *A History of Private Life*, vol. II: *Revelations of the Medieval World.* A. Goldhammer, trans. Cambridge, MA: Belknap Press.

Dunbabin, K. M. D. 2003. *The Roman Banquet: Images of Conviviality.* Cambridge: Cambridge University Press.

Erb, W. 1883. *Handbook of Electro-Therapeutics.* L. Putzel, trans. New York: William Wood.

Fairbairn, W. R. D. 1952. *Psychoanalytic Studies of the Personality.* London: Tavistock/Routledge.

Fairbairn, W. R. D. 1958. On the Nature and Aims of Psycho-analytic Treatment. *Int J Psychoanal* 39: 374–385.

Forel, A. 1906. *Hypnotism, or Suggestion and Psychotherapy: A Study of the Psychological, Psycho-Physiological and Therapeutic Aspects of Hypnotism.* Trans. from the 5th German edn. by H.W. Armit. London: Rebman.

Forrest, D. V. 2004. Elements of Dynamics III: The Face and the Couch. *J Amer Acad Psycho-anal and Dynamic Psychiatry* 32(3): 551–564.

Forrester, J. 1994. 'Mille e tre': Freud and Collecting. In J. Elsner and R. Cardinal, eds. *The Cultures of Collecting, 124–251.* London: Reaktion Books.

Fraser, A. 2006. *Love and Louis XIV: The Women in the Life of the Sun King.* New York: Anchor Books/Random House.

Freud, S. 1886. Preface to the Translation of Charcot's *Lectures on the Diseases of the Nervous System.* **SE** 1.

Freud, S. 1888. Hysteria. **SE** 1.

Freud, S. 1888–1889. Preface to the Translation of Bernheim's *Suggestion.* **SE** 1.

Freud, S. 1888–1892. Papers on Hypnotism and Suggestion: Editor's Introduction. **SE** 1.

Freud, S. 1889. Review of August Forel's *Hypnotism.* **SE** 1.

Freud, S. 1891. Hypnosis. **SE** 1.

Freud, S. 1892–1893. A Case of Successful Treatment by Hypnotism. **SE 1**.

Freud, S. 1892–1894. Preface and Footnotes to the Translation of Charcot's *Tuesday Lectures*. **SE 1**.

Freud, S. 1901. *The Psychopathology of Everyday Life: Forgetting, Slips* of *the Tongue, Bungled Actions, Superstitions and Errors*. **SE 6**.

Freud, S. 1904. Freud's Psycho-Analytic Procedure. **SE 7**.

Freud, S. 1910. Five Lectures on Psycho-Analysis. **SE 11**.

Freud, S. 1912. Recommendations to Physicians Practising Psycho-Analysis. **SE 12**.

Freud, S. 1913. On Beginning the Treatment. **SE 12**.

Freud, S. 1925. *An Autobiographical Study*. **SE 20**.

Friedberg, A., and Linn, L. 2012. The Couch as Icon. *Psychoanal Rev* 99(1): 35–62.

Fuss, D. 2004. *The Sense of an Interior: Four Writers and the Rooms that Shaped Them.* London: Routledge.

Gaddis, J. L. 2002. *The Landscape of History: How Historians Map the Past.* New York: Oxford University Press.

Gamwell, L., and Wells, R., eds. 1989. *Sigmund Freud and Art: His Personal Collection of Antiquities.* New York: Harry N. Abrams.

Gedo, J. E. 1995. Channels of Communication and the Analytic Setup. *Psychoanal Inq* 15: 294–303.

Gilman, S. L. 1993. *The Case of Sigmund Freud: Medicine and Identity at the Fin de Siècle.* Baltimore: Johns Hopkins University Press.

Gloag, J. 1966. *A Social History of Furniture Design: From B.C. 1300 to A.D. 1960.* New York: Bonanza Books.

Goldberger, M. 1995. The Couch as Defense and as Potential for Enactment. *Psychoanal Q* 64: 23–42.

Gowers, E. 2006. Lie-down Dinner. *Times Literary Supplement*, December 22 and 29, 2006, p. 7.

Greenacre, P. [1954] 1971. The Role of Transference: Practical Considerations in Relation to Psychoanalytic Therapy. In *Emotional Growth: Psychoanalytic Studies of the Gifted and a Great Variety of Other Individuals*, vol. 2, 627–640. New York: International Universities Press.

Greenberg, J. 2001. The Analyst's Participation: Response to Commentaries. *J Am Psychoanal Assoc* 49(2): 417–426.

Grier, K. C. 1988. *Culture and Comfort: Parlor Making and Middle-Class Identity, 1850–1930.* Washington: Smithsonian Institution Press.

Guntrip, H. 1975. My Experience of my Analysis with Fairbairn and Winnicott—(How complete a result does psycho-analytic therapy achieve?). *Int Rev Psychoanal* 2: 145–156.

References

Hanley, S. 1983. *The Lit de Justice of the Kings of France: Constitutional Ideology in Legend, Ritual, and Discourse.* Princeton: Princeton University Press.

Holt, M. P. 1988. The King in *Parlement*: The Problem of the *Lit de justice* in 16th-Century France. *Hist J* 31(3): 507–523.

Housholder, M. S. 1974. A Historical Perspective on the Obstetric Chair. *Surg Gynecol Obstet* 139: 423–430.

Jack, B. 2012. *The Woman Reader.* New Haven: Yale University Press.

Jacobson, J. G. 1995. The Analytic Couch: Facilitator or sine qua non? *Psychoanal Inq* 15: 304–313.

Kasson, J. F. 1990. *Rudeness and Civility: Manners in Nineteenth-Century Urban America.* New York: Hill & Wang.

Kellogg, J. H. 1910. *Light Therapeutics: A Practical Manual of Phototherapy for the Student and the Practitioner.* Battle Creek, MI: Good Health Publishing.

Kelman, H. 1954. The Use of the Analytic Couch. *Am J Psychoanal* 14: 65–82.

Kierkegaard, S. [1846] 1962. *The Present Age.* A. Dru, trans. New York: Harper Perennial.

Kirschner, S. R. 1996. *The Religious and Romantic Origins of Psychoanalysis: Individuation and Integration in Post-Freudian Theory.* Cambridge: Cambridge University Press.

Klauber, J. 1981. *Difficulties in the Analytic Encounter.* New York: Jason Aronson.

Kravis, N. 1988. James Braid's Psychophysiology: A Turning Point in the History of Dynamic Psychiatry. *Am J Psychiatry* 145(10): 1191–1206.

Kravis, N. 2013a. The Analyst's Hatred of Analysis. *Psychoanal Q* 82(1): 89–114.

Kravis, N. 2013b. *Fuck* Redux: A Review and Commentary. *J Am Psychoanal Assoc* 61(3): 527–534.

Kulish, N. 1996. A Phobia of the Couch: A Clinical Study of Psychoanalytic Process. *Psychoanal Q* 65: 465–494.

Kuspit, D. 1989. A Mighty Metaphor: The Analogy of Archaeology and Psychoanalysis. In L. Gamwell and R. Wells, eds. *Sigmund Freud and Art: His Personal Collection of Antiquities*, 133–151. New York: Harry N. Abrams.

Lable, I., Kelley, J. M., Ackerman, J., Levy, R., Waldron, S., and Ablon, J. S. 2010. The Role of the Couch in Psychoanalysis: Proposed Research Designs and Some Preliminary Data. *J Am Psychoanal Assoc* 58(5): 861–887.

LaFarge, L. 2000. Interpretation and Containment. *Int J Psychoanal* 81: 67–84.

Lichtenberg, J. D. 1995. Forty-five Years of Psychoanalytic Experiences on, behind, and without the Couch. *Psychoanal Inq* 15: 280–293.

Liddell, H. G., and Scott, R. [1871] 1935. *A Lexicon, Abridged from Liddell and Scott's Greek–English Lexicon.* Oxford: Clarendon Press.

Makari, G. 2008. *Revolution in Mind: The Creation of Psychoanalysis.* New York: HarperCollins.

Makari, G. 2015. *Soul Machine: The Invention of the Modern Mind.* New York: W. W. Norton.

Mayer, A. 2006. Lost Objects: From the Laboratories of Hypnosis to the Psychoanalytic Setting. *Sci Context* 19(1): 37–64.

Mayer, A. 2013. *Sites of the Unconscious: Hypnosis and the Emergence of the Psychoanalytic Setting.* Chicago: University of Chicago Press.

Midelfort, H. C. E. 1972. *Witch-Hunting in Southwestern Germany, 1582–1684.* Stanford: Stanford University Press.

Monell, S. H. 1900. *The Treatment of Disease by Electric Currents: A Handbook of Plain Instructions for the General Practitioner.* 2nd edn. New York: E. R. Pelton.

O'Donoghue, D. 2004. Negotiation of Surface: Archeology within the Early Strata of Psychoanalysis. *J Am Psychoanal Assoc* 52: 653–671.

Ogden, T. H. 1996. Reconsidering Three Aspects of Psychoanalytic Technique. *Int J Psychoanal* 77: 883–899.

Pardailhé-Galabrun, A. 1991. *The Birth of Intimacy: Privacy and Domestic Life in Early Modern Paris.* J. Phelps, trans. Philadelphia: University of Pennsylvania Press.

Perrot, M., ed. 1990. *A History of Private Life*, vol. 4: *From the Fires of Revolution to the Great War.* A. Goldhammer, trans. Cambridge, MA: Belknap Press/Harvard University Press.

Rieff, P. 1979. *Freud: The Mind of the Moralist*, 3rd edn. Chicago: University of Chicago Press.

Roazen, P. 1975. *Freud and His Followers.* New York: Knopf.

Robertiello, R. C. 1967. Two Views on the Use of the Couch: The Couch. *Psychoanal Rev* 54A: 69–71.

Rockwell, A. D. 1896. *The Medical and Surgical Uses of Electricity.* New York: William Wood.

Roller, M. B. 2006. *Dining Posture in Ancient Rome: Bodies, Values, and Status.* Princeton: Princeton University Press.

Roose, S. P. 2012. The Development of a Psychoanalytic Outcome Study: Choices, Conflicts, and Consensus. *J Am Psychoanal Assoc* 60(2): 311–335.

Roper, L. 2004. *Witch Craze: Terror and Fantasy in Baroque Germany.* New Haven: Yale University Press.

Rose, N. 1996. *Inventing Our Selves: Psychology, Power, and Personhood.* Cambridge: Cambridge University Press.

Ross, J. M. 1999. Once More onto the Couch: Consciousness and Preconscious Defenses in Psychoanalysis. *J Am Psychoanal Assoc* 47(1): 91–111.

Rudofsky, B. 1980. *Now I Lay Me Down to Eat: Notes and Footnotes on the Lost Art of Living.* Garden City, NY: Anchor Books.

Rybczynski, W. 1986. *Home: A Short History of an Idea.* New York: Viking.

Sadow, L. 1995. Looking, Listening, and the Couch. *Psychoanal Inq* 15: 386–395.

Said, E. W. 1978. *Orientalism.* New York: Random House.

Sarnitz, A., and Scholz-Strasser, I., eds. 2015. *Private Utopia: Cultural Setting of the Interior in the 19th and 20th Century*. Berlin: De Gruyter.

Schacter, J., and Kächele, H. 2010. The Couch in Psychoanalysis. *Contemp Psychoanal* 46: 439–459.

Schama, S. 1989. *Citizens: A Chronicle of the French Revolution*. New York: Knopf.

Sherwin, R. K. 2011. *Visualizing Law in the Age of the Digital Baroque: Arabesques and Entanglements*. London: Routledge.

Skolnick, N. J. 2015. Rethinking the Use of the Couch: A Relational Perspective. *Contemp Psychoanal* 51: 624–648.

Snodin, M., and Howard, M. 1996. *Ornament: A Social History since 1450*. New Haven: Yale University Press.

Speert, H. 1973. *Iconographica Gyniatrica: A Pictorial History of Gynecology and Obstetrics*. Philadelphia: F. A. Davis.

Stern, H. 1978. *The Couch: Its Use and Meaning in Psychotherapy*. New York: Human Sciences Press.

Swaan, A. de. 1977. On the Sociogenesis of the Psychoanalytic Setting. In P. B. Gleichmann, J. Goudsblom, and H. Korte, eds. *Human Figurations: Essays for Aufsätze für Norbert Elias*, 381–413. Amsterdam: Sociologisch Tijdschrift.

Swales, P. J. 1986. Freud, His Teacher, and the Birth of Psychoanalysis. In P. E. Stepansky, ed. *Freud: Appraisals and Reappraisals*, vol. 1, 3–82. Hillsdale, NJ: Analytic Press.

Talbott, P. 2002. Continuity and Innovation: Recliners, Sofa Beds, Rocking Chairs, and Folding Chairs. *Mag Antiq* 161(5): 124–133.

Thornton, P. 1984. *Authentic Décor: The Domestic Interior, 1620–1920*. New York: Viking Penguin.

Trevor-Roper H. R. 1969. *The European Witch-Craze of the Sixteenth and Seventeenth Centuries, and Other Essays*. New York: Harper & Row.

Verlet, P. 1991. *French Furniture of the Eighteenth Century*. P. Hunter-Stiebel, trans. Charlottesville: University Press of Virginia.

Warner, M. 2011. Freud's Couch: A Case History. *Raritan* 31(2): 146–163.

Winnicott, D. W. [1960] 1965. The Theory of the Parent–Infant Relationship. In *The Maturational Processes and the Facilitating Environment: Studies in the Theory of Emotional Development*, 37–55. Madison, CT: International Universities Press.

Wolf, E. S. 1995. Brief Notes on Using the Couch. *Psychoanal Inq* 15: 314–323.

Wright, L. 1962. *Warm and Snug: The History of the Bed*. London: Routledge & Kegan Paul.

Illustration Credits

3.1: The Metropolitan Museum of Art, New York, Fletcher Fund, 1924

3.2: The Metropolitan Museum of Art, New York, Gift of Samuel H. Kress Foundation, 1958

3.3: The Metropolitan Museum of Art, New York, Rogers Fund, 1920

3.4: The Metropolitan Museum of Art, New York, Gift of Mrs. Russell Sage, 1909

3.5: De Agostini Picture Library/A. C. Cooper/Bridgeman Images

3.6: Private collection/Bridgeman Images

3.7: De Agostini Picture Library/G. Dagli Orti/Getty Images

3.8: Victoria & Albert Museum, London/De Agostini Picture Library/A. C. Cooper/Bridgeman Images

3.9: The Metropolitan Museum of Art, New York, The Jack and Belle Linsky Collection, 1982

3.10: Fogg Art Museum, Harvard Art Museums, Cambridge, MA/Bequest of Grenville L. Winthrop/Bridgeman Images

3.11: Calmann & King Ltd/Bridgeman Images

4.1: Louvre, Paris/Bridgeman Images

4.2: Galleria Borghese, Rome/Bridgeman Images

4.3: © Staatliche Kunstsammlungen Dresden/Bridgeman Images

4.4: Cleveland Museum of Art, Ohio/Leonard C. Hanna, Jr. Fund/Bridgeman Images

4.5: J. T. Vintage/Bridgeman Images

4.6: The Metropolitan Museum of Art, New York, Gilman Collection, Purchase, The Horace W. Goldsmith Foundation Gift, through Joyce and Robert Menschel, 2005

4.7: Philadelphia Museum of Art, The William H. Helfand Collection, 1988-102-113

4.8: The Metropolitan Museum of Art, New York, Gift of Mrs. Bayard Verplanck, in memory of Dr. James Sykes Rumsey, 1940

4.9: The Metropolitan Museum of Art, New York, Gift of Mrs. Charles Reginald Leonard, in memory of Edgar Welch Leonard, Robert Jarvis Leonard, and Charles Reginald Leonard, 1957

4.10: The Metropolitan Museum of Art, New York, The Jack and Belle Linsky Collection, 1982

4.11: Courtesy of Perrin Antiquaires, Paris

4.12: Courtesy of Sotheby's

4.13: © RMN-Grand Palais/Art Resource, NY

4.14: De Agostini Picture Library/A. Dagli Orti/Bridgeman Images

4.15: Rijksmuseum, Netherlands

4.16: De Agostini Picture Library/Bridgeman Images

4.17: J. Paul Getty Museum, Los Angeles/Bridgeman Images

4.18: Author's collection

4.19: Museo Archeologico Nazionale, Naples, Italy/Bridgeman Images

4.20: Bridgeman Images

4.21: A. Dagli Orti/Bridgeman Images

4.22: Musée d'Orsay, Paris/Bridgeman Images

4.23: Hulton Archive/Fototeca Storica Nazionale/Getty Images

4.24: Musée d'Orsay, Paris/Bridgeman Images

4.25: Williams College Museum of Art, Gift of C. A. Wimpfheimer, Class of 1949

4.26: Tretyakov Gallery, Moscow/Sputnik/Bridgeman Images

4.27: Photo © Christie's Images/Bridgeman Images

4.28: National Gallery of Art, Washington, DC/Bridgeman Images

4.29: Museu de Montserrat, Abadia de Montserrat, Spain/Index/Bridgeman Images

4.30: Hulton Archive/Getty Images

4.31: The LIFE Picture Collection/Getty Images

4.32: Metropolitan Museum of Art, New York, Bequest of William K. Vanderbilt, 1920

4.33: Alte Pinakothek, Munich/Bridgeman Images

4.34: Photo © Les Arts Décoratifs, Paris/akg-images

4.35: Royal Museums of Fine Arts of Belgium, Brussels/photo: J. Geleyns

4.36: National Gallery of Art, Washington, DC/Bridgeman Images

4.37: Fontevrault Abbey, Fontevrault (Fontevraud), France/Bridgeman Images

4.38: Modern Art Museum of Fort Worth, Museum purchase, The Benjamin J. Tillar Memorial Trust, © 2012 Estate of Pablo Picasso/Artists Rights Society (ARS), New York; Tom Jenkins

5.1: De Agostini Picture Library/A. Dagli Orti/Bridgeman Images

5.2: © The Frick Collection

5.3: The Stapleton Collection/Bridgeman Images

5.4: Hirshhorn Museum & Sculpture Garden, Washington, DC/Bridgeman Images

5.5: Image courtesy of Sotheby's

5.6: © The Museum of Modern Art/Licensed by SCALA/Art Resource, NY

5.7: Indianapolis Museum of Art, Gift of Alan Hartman

5.8: Metropolitan Museum of Art, New York, H. O. Havemeyer Collection, Bequest of Mrs. H. O. Havemeyer, 1929

5.9: Lee Friedlander/Fraenkel Gallery, San Francisco

5.10: Galleria degli Uffizi, Florence/Bridgeman Images

5.11: © RMN-Grand Palais/Art Resource, NY

5.12: Library of Congress, Prints and Photographs Division, Washington, DC

5.13: Author's collection

5.14: Author's collection

5.15: Library of Congress, Prints and Photographs Division, Washington, DC

5.16: © Look and Learn/Elgar Collection/Bridgeman Images

5.17: Archives Charmet/Bridgeman Images

5.18: Author's collection

5.19: Courtesy of the New York Academy of Medicine Library

5.20: Author's collection

5.21: BASF Corporate History

5.22: The Wellcome Library, London

5.23: The Stapleton Collection/Bridgeman Images

5.24: Author's collection

5.25: Author's collection

5.26: Author's collection

5.27: The Wellcome Library, London

5.28: The Wellcome Library, London

5.29: The Wellcome Library, London

5.30: The Fleet Library, Rhode Island School of Design

5.31: © F.L.C./ADAGP, Paris/Artists Rights Society (ARS), New York, 2017

5.32: Library of Congress, Prints and Photographs Division, Washington, DC

5.33: Author's collection

5.34: Author's collection

5.35: De Agostini Picture Library/G. Cigolini/Bridgeman Images

5.36: Library of Congress, Prints and Photographs Division, Washington, DC

6.1: Author's collection

6.2: The Bakken Library and Museum, Minneapolis, MN

6.3: © Look and Learn/Bridgeman Images

6.4: Author's collection

6.5: Author's collection

6.6: Author's collection

6.7: The Oskar Diethelm Library, DeWitt Wallace Institute for the History of Psychiatry, Weill Cornell Medical College, New York

6.8: The Oskar Diethelm Library, DeWitt Wallace Institute for the History of Psychiatry, Weill Cornell Medical College, New York

6.9: Author's collection

6.10: Author's collection

6.11: Author's collection

6.12: Picture Collection, The New York Public Library, Astor, Lenox and Tilden Foundations

7.1: The Freud Museum, London/Bridgeman Images

7.2: Robert Mankoff/The New Yorker Collection/The Cartoon Bank

7.3: The Freud Museum, London

7.4: The Wolfsonian Collection, Florida International University, Miami Beach, Florida

7.5: The Wolfsonian Collection, Florida International University, Miami Beach, Florida

7.6: Author's collection

7.7: Library of Congress, Prints and Photographs Division, Washington, DC

7.8: RKD–Nederlands Institut voor Kunstgeschiedenis

7.9: Cleveland Museum of Art, Ohio/John L. Severance Fund/Bridgeman Images

7.10: The Fleet Library, Rhode Island School of Design

8.1: Photograph by Dan Welldon, 2005, used with permission

8.2: Photograph by Jerome Blackman, 2016, used with permission

8.3: Photograph by Shellburne Thurber, 2000, used with permission

8.4: Author's collection

8.5: Freud Museum, London/Bridgeman Images

8.6: Sigmund Freud Copyrights, London

8.7: Authenticated News/Getty Images

8.8: J. C. Duffy/The New Yorker Collection/The Cartoon Bank

8.9: *Innen Dekoration*, 1903, p. 106

8.10: *Innen Dekoration*, 1902, p. 312

8.11: Musée Fabre, Montpellier, France/Bridgeman Images

8.12: Photo © Collection Bourgeron/Bridgeman Images

8.13: *Innen Dekoration*, 1902, p. 292

8.14: *Innen Dekoration*, 1902, p. 166

8.15: Lessing Images, Museo Nazionale Romano Inv. 61586, DAI Rome 80.2718

8.16: Photograph by Dan Welldon, 2007, used with permission

8.17: Photograph by Shellburne Thurber, 2000, used with permission

8.18: Photograph by Robert Tyson, 2002, used with permission

8.19: IPA Newsletter 2000; 9(2), p. 36

8.20: Photograph by Shellburne Thurber, 2000, used with permission

8.21: Photograph by Claudia Guderian, 2002, used with permission

9.1: Author's collection

9.2: Kachelhoffer Clement/Getty Images

9.3: Bruce Eric Kaplan/The New Yorker/© Condé Nast

9.4: Lee Lorenz/The New Yorker Collection/The Cartoon Bank

9.5: Photography Collection, Miriam and Ira D. Wallace Division of Art, Prints and Photographs, The New York Public Library, Astor, Lenox and Tilden Foundations

9.6: Author's collection

194

Index

Page numbers in italics indicate illustrations.

198